THE LEFT HAND PATH
PHILOSOPHY & PRAXIS

VOLUME I

Draco Press
© 2019 Edited by Asenath Mason & Bill Duvendack.
All rights reserved.
"The Left Hand Path: Philosophy & Praxis. Vol I"

Cover, Layout & Art: Asenath Mason

THE LEFT HAND PATH
PHILOSOPHY & PRAXIS

VOLUME I

Edited by
Asenath Mason & Bill Duvendack

Draco Press

2019

Table of Contents

Adam and Eve and the Tree of Knowledge
Jacob Rueff, XVI century

Introduction

Essays gathered in this book were written by members of Lodge Magan in the years 2002-2010 and are derived from Dragon's Blood magazine and other publications that were originally released at that time. The majority of them have an introductory character, explaining the basics of the Left Hand Path and its concepts, as such was their purpose when they were released for the first time, but there are also essays that refer to less known esoteric subjects.

Lodge Magan, located in Poland, was active in the years 2002-2012. Originally, it was a part of Dragon Rouge, a Scandinavian magical order dedicated to Draconian magic in its various aspects and manifestations. In 2009 members of Lodge Magan separated from the order and decided to continue the work as an active ritual circle, releasing many books, magazines and publications distributed worldwide. During those years Lodge Magan held regular meetings and open lectures, working with a variety of projects, which included such areas as witchcraft, necromancy, demonology, Goetic magic, Necronomicon Gnosis, and Qliphothic Qabalah, as well as many magical traditions: Egyptian, Persian, Greek, Scandinavian, and Babylonian. With the completion of the Eleven Qliphothic Powers of Tiamat, and after ten years of active work, the goals that had been set up for Lodge Magan and offside projects that arose in the meantime were accomplished and the work was considered as finished. The Lodge closed by the end of 2012, giving way to the Temple of Ascending Flame - founded on December 21st, 2012, by Asenath Mason.

With the growing interest in the Draconian Tradition and self-initiatory LHP magic, we have decided to revise this material and make it available again. We dedicate this book to all our readers, members of the Temple of Ascending Flame, and all who have supported our projects since 2012. We hope that you will find these texts interesting and inspiring in your personal work.

Asenath Mason & Bill Duvendack

The Path of Cain

Asenath Mason

"Now the serpent was more subtle than any beast of the field which the Lord God had made. And he said unto the woman, Yea, hath God said, Ye shall not eat of every tree of the garden? And the woman said unto the serpent, We may eat of the fruit of the trees of the garden: But of the fruit of the tree which is in the midst of the garden, God hath said, Ye shall not eat of it, neither shall ye touch it, lest ye die. And the serpent said unto the woman, Ye shall not surely die: For God doth know that in the day ye eat thereof, then your eyes shall be opened, and ye shall be as gods, knowing good and evil." (Genesis 3:1-5)

The Serpent in the Garden of Eden was Satan, God's Adversary, whose promise given to the first humans showed them the way to liberty, the path that leads not to the unity with God but to individual self-deification. Sometimes the Serpent is identified with Samael, sometimes with Lilith – both mythical characters who rebelled against God's orders and chose an independent way. However, it was not Adam or Eve themselves who followed their example, but their offspring. It is believed that the forbidden fruit which the first couple tasted was the sexual act. This is the claim of representatives of certain Gnostic sects, such as e.g. the Cathars. Peter Garcias wrote in 13th century that "The fruit forbidden to our ancestors was nothing else than a pleasure of a carnal intercourse." Another scholar, Egbert, wrote that the fruit which God did not allow to eat was "the woman he had created." God told Adam to refrain from an intercourse with her, but he did not listen, and this was the tasting of the forbidden fruit.

The first children born to Adam and Eve after their exile from the Garden of Eden were Abel and Cain. The origin of Cain is very ambiguous both in the Bible and in early Christian doctrines. Many of them question Adam's fatherhood and imply that Cain was conceived in a union of Eve with the Serpent. Moreover, at the same time Eve was reputedly possessed by Lilith, which makes Cain the son of Satan and Lilith. The Bible itself claims that Cain "was of that wicked one" (1 John 3:12) while Abel was the righteous son of Adam. They were both farmers and they both made offerings to God from the fruits of their labour: "Cain brought of the fruit of the ground an offering unto the Lord. And Abel brought the firstlings of his flock and of the fat thereof. And the Lord had respect unto Abel and to his offering: But unto Cain and to his offering he had not respect." (Genesis 4:3-5)

God accepted the bloody offering of Abel who sacrificed the first-born lamb from his herd, but he spurned the gift of Cain who brought the fruit and crops harvested from his fields. This made Cain angry and he killed his brother when they both went out on a field. God condemned Cain's deed and said to him: "What hast thou done? The voice of thy brother's blood crieth unto me from the ground. And now art thou cursed from the earth, which hath opened her mouth to receive thy brother's blood from thy hand." He banished Cain and cursed him to eternal exile, and he cannot die or rest from the weariness of life, for "whosoever slayeth Cain, vengeance shall be taken on him sevenfold. And the Lord set a mark upon Cain, lest any finding him should kill him. And Cain went out from the presence of the Lord, and dwelt in the land of Nod, on the east of Eden." (Genesis 4)

After Abel's death and Cain's exile, Adam once again approached his wife and she gave him a son whom she called Seth, saying that "God hath appointed me another seed instead of Abel, whom Cain slew." (Genesis 4:25) Since that time mankind divided into the offspring of Cain (the son of the Serpent) and the offspring of Adam (son of God). This division, however, is again very ambiguous. Many researchers of the Bible claim that even though Cain was the first-born son of Eve, he and Abel were conceived at the same time. In the moment of conception Samael's semen was mixed with Adam's. Thus, Cain inherited the qualities of the Serpent, Abel – those of man. Therefore, the birth of Seth should be regarded as the establishment of a bloodline uncontaminated by the Serpent's semen.

Cain had numerous offspring. His first-born son was Enoch. When Cain founded a city, he named it after him. Enoch was the father of Irad, Irad begat Mehujael, Mehujael begat Mehusael, and Mehusael begat Lamech. Lamech had two wives – Adah gave birth to Jabal, the pre-father of nomads and shepherds, and also to Jubal, the inventor of music and arts. His second wife Zillah gave birth to Tubal-Cain, the precursor of all blacksmiths, inventor of all tools from brass and iron. The daughter of Zillah and Lamech was Naamah. Among Cain's descendants were creators of all civilization on the earth. As they were denied the entrance to the Garden of Eden, by their work they tried to establish their own "paradise" where they could shape and create, i.e. to replace God. The Cainites, the name referring to the descendants and followers of Cain, soon created their own civilization which is represented by three sons of Lamech: Tubal-Cain (crafts), Jubal (music and arts) and Jabal (agriculture). Thus, the descendants of Cain established the line whose members took care of the most important domains, both material (craftsmanship, the production of food), as well as spiritual (music, poetry, etc.). Their culture progressed and flourished very fast, and it is said in the Bible: "for the children of this world are in their generation wiser than the children of Light." (Lucas 16:8)

Cain, who shaped his own fate, is therefore the emblem of the way isolated from God and his laws. In his pursuit of self-salvation or self-deification he became the precursor of the spiritual path which later was named the Left Hand Path. He does not accept his curse, according to which he was supposed to be merely an outcast and a wanderer, and he becomes the symbol of all progress that occurs outside the world created by God. He is the first to build a city and he creates his own world, independent from God. He rebels against God's judgment and he tries to decide about his destiny himself. His way is the path of self-salvation, the defeat of the curse and the rebellious separation from God, the pursuit of self-deification in order to shape his own Garden of Eden, without God and imposed laws.

The name of the first city founded by Cain, "Enoch," means "dedicated" and it refers to a dedication to a new beginning, separation from the past and the act of entering the way independent from all "higher forces," laws and orders. The way of Abel and the descendants of Adam/Seth is the Right Hand Path, the pursuit of reconstruction of the original order in order to recover the place in the divine Garden of Eden from which mankind was banished, and the dream of a reunion with God the Father and the eternal life in his Light. The path of Cain is the Left Hand Path which strives to create one's own world, to one's own self-deification. It is the faith in one's own possibilities and the potential of flesh and the world in which man lives. Erich Sauer writes: "The supreme fulfillment of 'Abel' is Christ and through him the embodiment (i.e. humanization) of the holy God. The supreme form of 'Cain' is the Antichrist and through him the self-worship of the damned man."

Cain and Abel
From *Complete Works of Lord Byron,* illustrated by Charles
Mettais, Bocourt and Gustave Doré, 1853

Cain is one of the first initiators of the Left Hand Path and
the first of humans who made a conscious choice of his
path and has walked it ever since, without any hesitation.
His way leads to the fulfillment of the promise given by the

Serpent to Eve and Adam in the Garden of Eden. The murder of his brother Abel is a symbolic defeat of the weak half of consciousness. Samael, Lilith and their child Cain constitute the triad which signifies the initiatory model of the first stage on the way to self-deification. On the Qliphothic Tree of Night they correspond to the levels of Gamaliel (the lunar sphere of the goddess Lilith, mother of all demons), Samael (the Qlipha related to the concept of the shadow Serpent-Initiator), and Thagirion (the central level on the Tree of Night, related to the child of the infernal couple). Therefore, there is a relation between Cain and the Antichrist who also corresponds to the sphere of Thagirion and who is the central character on the path of separation from God as well as the archetypal initiator. Cain is the first human who awakened the inner spark of divinity which may be transformed into the flame of immortality. This is the fire which nurtures and strengthens, burning all human weaknesses and transforming man into god.

Cain as a character is surrounded by many controversial theories suggested by the Bible researchers as well as common readers. There are many legends and tales in which he is described as an embodiment of all evil and the son of the Devil. He was supposed to indulge in sexual relations with his mother (Lilith), to practice cannibalism and to drink Abel's blood, which made him a popular symbol of vampirism in modern times. Legends depict him as the one who invented murder, incited conflicts, introduced war and rebellion into the world, and became the lord of envy and greed. His offering was rejected by God because it contained the worst crops of all he had. He and his mother Lilith were the evil that was the reason for the Flood because it was him who begat monsters born by Lilith. It is even said that Cain had horns just like his devilish father. One of his descendants, Naamah, is regarded in demonology as Lilith's alter ego and she has demonic aspects. It is often said that the descendants of Cain entered incestuous relationships. Cain's marriage itself is quite mysterious. Not much is known about his wife. Sometimes she is believed to be his sister, as the Old Testament mentions numerous sons and daughters of Adam and Eve. Thus, perhaps Cain and Abel, the first-born sons, simply married their younger sisters.

In the Jewish Encyclopedia we read about Cain:

"Cain is the type of avarice, of 'folly and impiety' and of self-love. 'He built a city' means that 'he built a doctrinal system of lawlessness, insolence, and immoderate indulgence in pleasure;' and the Epicurean philosophers are of the school of Cain, claiming to have Cain as teacher and guide, who recommended the worship of the sensual powers in preference to the powers above, and who practised his doctrine by destroying Abel, the expounder of the opposite doctrine."

In Christian apocryphal literature and some Jewish sources, the daughters of Cain are the ones who seduced "the sons of God" and caused their fall. This tale is interpreted as the union of Cain's daughters with the sons of Seth – the demonic descendants of Samael with humans, the worshippers of Jahweh. But there is another interpretation in which the fallen "sons of God" are the angels who descended to the earth in order to join in a sexual union with women. The fallen angels taught their partners magic and all mystical arts which had been reserved to God and angels until that moment. From this union the daughters of Cain bore the so called "giants," the symbol of a brutal force and inhuman power. Lilith taught their daughters all forms of debauchery, and she showed the sons of god how to cloak the soul with flesh and obtain sensual delight. The daughters of Cain, just like Lilith herself, were the initiators of carnal pleasures obtained from sexual acts which led the sons of God to debauchery and sin. This resulted in wild orgies at the foot of the mountain near Eden, accompanied by the music invented by Jubal. None of those who joined them returned to God's mercy and remained in sin forever. Similar practices are ascribed to the Gnostic sect named "Cainites:"

"In the second century of the common era a Gnostic sect by the name of 'Cainites' is frequently mentioned as forming a branch of the antinomistic heresies which, adopting some of the views of Paulinian Christianity, advocated and practised indulgence in carnal pleasure. While some of the Jewish Gnostics divided men into three classes - represented (1) by Cain, the physical or earthly man; (2) by Abel, the psychical man (the middle class); and (3) by Seth, the spiritual or saintly man - the antinomistic pagan Gnostics declared Cain and other rebels or sinners to be their prototypes of evil and licentiousness. Cain, Esau, Korah, the Sodomites, and even Judas Iscariot, were made by these Gnostics expounders of the 'wisdom' of the serpent in rebellion against God." *(The Jewish Encyclopedia)*

The Cainites were therefore not only the biblical descendants of Cain but also the name of an antinomian Gnostic sect. Like other groups of this kind (the Ophites, the Naassenes, etc.), they believed the God of the Old Testament is in fact the "God of Evil" and the Serpent in the Garden of Eden was the savior who brought humans salvation. Thus, they thought that all characters presented in the Old Testament as evil in fact were personifications of good. Cain as the first man who rebelled against God, was of special significance. They had a similar attitude to Esau, Korah, Noah's raven, or the inhabitants of Sodom and Gomorrah. Among the characters from the New Testament they preferred Mary Magdalene to the Virgin Mary, as well as Simon Magus and Judas. They reverted biblical values and claimed that the evil characters were the advocates of

Gnosis, the true esoteric knowledge. The Cainites believed that God must be bloodthirsty and evil if he accepted Abel's bloody sacrifice and rejected crops gifted by Cain. They thought that it is the path of Cain not of Abel that leads to salvation and eternal life, not in union with God, but in self-salvation. To break the laws and rules of the Old Testament was regarded as a duty because this was the only way to achieve perfection and save the soul from eternal darkness. They also believed that salvation might be achieved when one experiences everything in the world. Epiphanius describes the Cainites as a group indulging in licentious and impious acts in worship of numerous deities. In many sources they are labeled as the worshippers of Satan.

The city of Enoch, the symbol of civilization established by Cain, is by many early Christian philosophers regarded as the seat of diseases, violence, debauchery and sin. It was a huge industrial and cultural center. Many merchants traveled there. Trade and crafts flourished. The city had its own laws, for which it was labeled as the seat of sin because it did not attract those who sought a pious life but people came there in search of pleasures and satisfaction. Saint Augustine wrote that it was the opposite of Jerusalem, the city founded by God. Cain's city represented the earth, the realm of matter and senses; Jerusalem – the spiritual world, the celestial realm free of sin. Cain's civilization is identified with the most ancient kingdoms and societies, especially the Babylonian and Assyrian cultures. He is regarded as the builder of such cities as Nineveh, Evech, Agade, Lagash, and of course Babylon – one of the most important "devilish cities" in the Bible. His civilization includes also such cities as Sodom and Gomorrah, the famous biblical emblems of corruption.

Some Qabalistic theories are, however, far from identifying Cain only with the principle of evil. A significant function is ascribed to this character by the Lurianic Kabbalah. According to this theory, the souls of Cain and Abel are two complementary sides of the divine principle. Cain belongs to the left emanations on the Tree of Life (Adam's "left shoulder" – the sephira Din), while Abel descends from his father's right shoulder (Chesed). Gerschom Scholem even claims that when all souls will be restored, "Cain will be infinitely higher than Abel." He is the symbol of a higher consciousness which contains divine qualities within, while Abel is the lower consciousness which through his blood returns to the earth. The name "Abel" (Hevel) itself stems from the Hebrew words meaning "to breathe," "to blow," "to be vain," "transitory," which implies the transience of his nature. He is merely a transitory form of consciousness, the higher form of which is Cain (Qaheen). According to the Lurianic Kabbalah, all souls will descend from theirs. Here Cain is not the son of the Devil but an incarnation of God himself (YHWH).

The mysterious "mark" which God put on Cain while banishing him from his presence is often thought to be the mark of "the Beast" that heralds the Apocalypse. This is associated with Cain's role as the Antichrist who embodies the concept of salvation without God, the antinomian path of self-deification. "The mark of Cain" is also sometimes believed to be a horn which grows out of his forehead, the sign of his devilish nature. In another interpretation, it is an imprint which was formed when Cain's forehead was hit by the jewel from the crown of falling Lucifer. There is also a theory that the mark is the sign of the Red Serpent, and one more which associates Cain with Saturn (the Devil's planet) and in which the mark has the form of a six-rayed star or the TAU cross. But the mark is not actually a visible sign but rather a symbol of an awakened consciousness, "magical imprint," a spark of divinity which evokes in a human soul anxiety and insatiable longing for knowledge and power, "the spiritual desire of sin." This anxiety tempts man to seek one's own divinity and leads onto the path of Cain. It is thought that adepts who bear "the mark of Cain" are his descendants, followers on the initiatory path which was begun by him. The mark of Cain is therefore the opposite of "the sign of God" given to those who follow divine laws. Being marked with it signifies the rebellion against God and his orders. Adepts on the path of Cain are therefore deprived of God's protection and must rely only on themselves and their own strength. That is why it is also a path which demands a great deal of responsibility, persistence and dedication.

"Woe unto them! for they have gone in the way of Cain." (Jude 11)

Bibliography:

1. David Williams: *Cain and Beowulf*
2. Kaufmann Kohler, W.H. Bennet, Louis Ginzberg: *The Jewish Encyclopedia*
3. Gershom Scholem: *On the Mystical Shape of the Godhead*
4. Israel Regardie: *The Golden Dawn*
5. The Bible: all quotations from King James Version
6. Jean Duvernoy: *Catharism, the History of the Cathars,*
7. Erich Sauer: *Dwie drogi ludzkości*

Invocation of the Adversary

Daemon V.

This ritual was designed for a solitary practitioner, the traveler in search of knowledge who seeks to awaken the essence of the Adversary in their inner mind. Decorate your ritual space with black colors. On the altar put an image of Samael – this can be a statue or picture, either of Samael, Melek Taus, or Adramelek. This can also be an image of Baphomet. Prepare a chalice and fill it with a strong liquid – black, red or purple, the symbol of Samael's poison. Face the altar and gaze into the image of the god. Repeat his name as a mantra, mentally or aloud, and focus on how the atmosphere in the temple thickens. When you feel the air is electrified with the energy, begin the ritual.

Face North and speak the words:

From the black abysses within the bowels of the earth, I call you, Belial! Arise and come forth! May darkness fill my temple of flesh!

Facing West:

From the infinite sea of darkness, I call you, Timeless Serpent! Leviathan, arise and come forth! May the black ocean of dreams reveal to me its secrets!

Facing South:

From the fiery realms of lust and fornication, I call you, Satan! Arise and come forth! May the black flame consume the weakness in my heart!

Facing East:

From the eternal dawn of time, I call you, Morning Star! Lucifer, arise and come forth! May the rays of the Black Sun engulf my mind as the light of illumination!

Facing the altar:

The gates are open wide and the creatures of the night are coming on the wings of darkness!

SAMAEL! ADRAMELEK! SHEMAL! SAKLAS! HVHI!

NEMA OLAM A SON AREBIL DES MENOITATNET NI SACUDNI SON EN TE SIRTSON SUBIROTIBED SUMITTIMID SON TE TUCIS ARTSON ATIBED SIBON ETTIMID TE EIDOH SIBON AD MUNAIDITOUQ MURTSON MENAP ARRET NI TE OLEAC NI TUCIS AUT SATNULOV TAIF MUUT MUNGER TAINEVDA MUUT NEMON RUTECIFITCNAS SILEAC NI SE IUQ RETSON RETAP

I call you, eternal Accuser and Destroyer!
You, who walks between the worlds and transcends all boundaries and limitations!
Come to my temple of flesh!
Appear before me, Angel of Death and Destruction!
Let me into your garden of insanity and dark wisdom!
Annihilate the world of illusion and stagnation and lead me to freedom and illumination!
Eternal Seducer, tempt me with the Fruits of Knowledge

For I am the one who is not afraid to taste them!
Lead me through the gates of lust into your kingdom of
ecstasy!
Show me the light in darkness!
Teach me the ways of creation and destruction
So that I may die and create myself again as a god!

SAMAEL! ADRAMELEK! SHEMAL! SAKLAS! HVHI!

I become as you: wise, willful, and powerful!
My eyes gaze into all dimensions of eternity!
My voice permeates the vast blackness of the whole
universe!
I spread my rainbow wings
And laugh at the petty knowledge of humans!
I am the Poison of God and I hold the chalice with the
elixir of life and death,
I am the Angel of Death and the wrath of eternity,
I am the Prince of Hell and the consort of Lilith in the
timeless embrace of the Great Serpent,
I am the Father of Lies and I shake the foundations of the
world so that it may fall and rise again,
I am the Primeval Spirit of Evil and the Shadow of
Creation,
And I am the Lord of the World!

I am Samael!

Dark Princess Naamah

Adam

"And two female spirits - Lilith and Naamah - would come and copulate with him and bear children. And those whom they bore are the evil spirits of the world who are called the Plagues of Mankind." *(Zohar)*

She is called by many different names and worshipped as a goddess of many faces. Naamah – the ruler of the first Qlipha on the Tree of Night is the one who mounts the Beast. She is the serpent lurking by the Tree of Life and waiting to climb on its top, the one "from above" or "from beyond." Her name is most often translated as "Pleasant," for in the Hebrew tradition she "sang pleasant songs to idols." However, due to her connection to the kingdom of the night, shadows and phantoms, she is also called "Groaning," as the creatures over whom she presides are traditionally responsible for strange and terrifying sounds in the night, awakening dark desires in men and leading them astray from God. Naamah is also believed to be the mother of divination, whose talent was not surpassed by any other, and the sister of Tubal Cain. She is known for her artistic talents, especially those concerning music instruments and singing, and she is the force contained within the realm of matter.

"Beautiful"

"And this Naamah became aroused and adhered to her evil side. And to this day she exists, and her abode is among the waves of the great sea. And she comes forth, and makes sport with the sons of man, and becomes hot from them in the dream, in that desire which a man has, and she clings to him, and she takes the desire and from it she conceives and brings forth other kinds of spirits into the world."

The character of Naamah is most often analyzed in the category of a succubus, a vampiric spirit haunting men at night in order to drain their vital sexual essences during a perverse intercourse. In the Zoharic Qabalah, the goddess is viewed as an angel of prostitution and one of Samael's consorts, mentioned alongside Eisheth Zenunim, Agrat Bat Mahlat, or Lilith herself. Perhaps her stunning beauty, which she uses to seduce men in their night visions, is the reason why she is also called "Beautiful." According to the apocrypha, she joined Lilith in haunting Adam when he and Eve separated for one hundred and thirty years after Cain's murder of Abel because he did not want to beget children in the world of fear and violence. Demonic offspring born from this union are called the Plagues of Mankind because they lead humans away from God. But the goddess also reputedly visits each man filled with lust, giving birth to hundreds of other dark entities.

But what exactly are the demons born from the union of a mortal man with the dark princess Naamah? These are dreams, fantasies and desires which underlie the structures of the material world, yet remaining hidden and unconscious. In this sense, the waves of the great sea from which the goddess comes become the ocean of the unconscious, the sea of forces on which a small part of our consciousness drifts, exposed to interaction with the mundane world. These forces are believed to lead us away from God because they are a projection of our personal aspirations and pursuits - attempts to create our own perfect paradise hidden from conscious awareness. They represent the shackles of the material world – the imprisonment in lusts and ambitions which do not lead anywhere, depriving us of energy and satisfaction with what we already have. They are the pillars on which we build our subjective image of reality. This projection of unconscious aspirations often assumes a sexual form, like it is in the case of the possessive urge, and so the demons of Naamah and the goddess herself also manifest with a lot of sexual imagery. Still beyond our awareness, these energies bind our existence and keep it addicted to the materialistic view of the surrounding world.

And thus, when we confront Naamah, we face our urges and sources of motivation which shape our actions in the mundane life. On the one hand, we open ourselves to all unusual desires and aspirations, gaining new will and joy of life. On the other hand, when we start to realize why we actually act the way we do, why we desire things, we are on a good way to liberate ourselves from them. By reaching to the source of urges we can satisfy and use them for a conscious action. Naamah is said to endow the magician with all pleasures and riches of the world, and it is so indeed. But if this meant indulgence in material goods, we would be bound even more to the sphere of matter instead of being liberated from the shackles of the world. The way to true spiritual progress is far from any dualism. Heaven and hell are within us and the "riches of the world" are only a tool to perceive and experience the material plane in a conscious and chosen way. That is why Naamah is called "Beautiful" – for she shows us the true beauty which emanates onto the material world from the center of our existence.

"Pleasant" and "Groaning"

"Yobal made reed instruments, and harps, and flutes, and whistles, and the devils went and dwelt inside them. When men blew into the pipes, the devils sang inside them."

The joy of life and satisfaction with living in harmony with oneself are reflected in another aspect of Naamah's character. As we have already observed, the goddess was also called "Pleasant." The followers of Cain, after being exiled from the Garden of Eden, had to conquer the hostile world and create their own space on the earth. This was the beginning of civilization, with its technical achievements, culture and arts. While Tubal Cain was the inventor of technical advancement – the symbolic first blacksmith and craftsman – his sister Naamah surpassed everyone with her talent for musical instruments and singing. Monotheistic religions saw the joy of life expressed by music, sexual intercourse or singing as sinful, i.e. distracting man from following the way of God. This was because such elements led to affirmation of life and its power and encouraged man to seek happiness in himself, not in a mere expectation of reward in a distant, abstract world which is available only in the afterlife. Moreover, the aversion to ecstatic music and pagan folklore was caused by the fact that music was used as a ritual tool, connected with the conviction that the spirit of a deity inhabited the instrument and spoke to the priest through the sound. This spirit could also be controlled by means of special music. What is interesting is that a familiar spirit ascribed to the famous witch of Endor was an old lifeless instrument, made from an old goatskin.

But this view on the nature of music also implies a deeper esoteric meaning. This refers to the interpretation of Naamah's name as "Groaning." On the one hand, Naamah's music represents all tones, vibrations and dark energies that are channeled when we begin out first initiatory practices with the Lilith Qlipha, the first level on the Tree of Night. This is a particular opening up for darkness and its transformative aspects. Perhaps for this reason, the nature of music itself is so fascinating and connected with the chaotic sphere of the Qliphothic Tree – our mind is not capable of classifying the sounds, it can merely create a map of correlations between the tones, which makes it subjective for everyone. On the other hand, this can refer to the method of summoning and communicating with the forces, which occurs by means of music and voice as well as by a trance induced by sounds. In antiquity, a word was considered powerful in itself, and knowledge of a true name of things was believed to give control over them. This is reflected in certain myths of creation in patriarchal religions, such as e.g. the Mesopotamian or the Hebrew lore in which Jehova and Marduk create things by naming them. And even though today we do not pay attention to the meaning of our words, it is a great mistake to underrate their power. Our mind is able to register and process only a small percentage of impulses which reach it in each second, so the words we use to describe the surrounding reality are enormously important. The language influences our perception, and by using a certain meaning, tone and style we create our own tunnel of reality. In other words – by defining the world around we can shape our lives.

It is also worth mentioning that while music and words are used to make contact and achieve the understanding of energies and vibrations, the deeper exploration of this method might lead us to a deeper understanding of the structure and their role in the universe. Perhaps for this reason Naamah is believed to be the Mother of Divination. Through ability to achieve a trance and a concrete medium, as well as through continual broadening of our mental capabilities, through a profound insight into the nature of ourselves and the world around us, we can gain the ability to predict the direction of our tunnel of reality and predict future events. In a similar way we can learn to contact and manipulate the subtle currents of astral energies which in fact are the forces that constitute the foundation of the material plane.

"Sleeping"

"And all went astray after them. And there was one male who came into the world from the spirit of Cain's side, and they called Tubal-Cain. And a female came forth with him, and the creatures went astray after her, and her name was Naamah. From her issued other spirits and demons."

We shall now discuss the nature of Naamah in the context of the antinomian Left Hand Path. As Tubal Cain's sister, she might represent the female completion of the path of isolation and separation from the natural order. Here we can again refer to her name which was also attributed to a town, as it is mentioned in the Book of Joshua. If we connect it with the fact that the tribe of Cain was the first to create cities on earth, we can reach some interesting conclusions. It can be therefore a metaphor of isolation of one's consciousness – a complete and independent city, opposed to the rest of the "natural" world ruled by God. In this sense, Naamah's name attributed to the city (not exactly the city in question but in general understanding) may become a complementary crowning of the path, enriching it with the feminine element. This hypothesis might be confirmed by certain correlations achieved by the art of Gematria and the Qabalah in which the numerical analysis of this concept would leave us with words such as "Palace," "Gathering," or "Little City." Also the reference to Malkuth, the first sephira on the Tree of Life, equivalent to the Lilith Qlipha, which means "Kingdom," might give us some clues to further understanding of the issue.

The left, female side is also connected with many other conceptions related to Naamah. Her symbolism refers to other basic aspects that belong to the left hand path of spiritual development. Because of her attributes, the goddess is often associated with the realm of the night and nocturnal animals, which suggests a metaphoric allusion to the element of darkness. This is the transformative element in nature which allows for all progress and movement. It is the alchemical process of *Solve* by which the old elements are destroyed to make place for the new – evolution and regeneration. It should be stressed, however, that conceptions of light and darkness in this paradigm are not marked with any moral characteristics – they are complementary forces which allow for the existence of the universe in itself. There has to be a force that brings death and destruction so that creation might be possible. Like all other Qliphothic energies, Naamah is associated with the principles of chaos and destruction – as we have already observed – she is the force that challenges us on a particular level and liberates us from the shackles of the world so that we can enter a higher level and confront other ordeals on the path toward ultimate freedom.

But darkness is not only death and destruction. Female deities, often black and associated with the impregnated earth, were also symbolic of fertility and the primeval waters of chaos. The motif of creation of the world from the ocean of prime matter is common to many pagan mythologies. It also represents the transcendence of dualisms connected with life and death – the collection of all potentialities – the place from which all creation emerges and returns after the end of the mundane life. The female element, connected with darkness, the night, and mystical waters, is also associated with the symbolism of the moon. This is viewed as an analogy between the female menstrual cycle, related to the moon phases and natural tides. The moon is the symbol of eternal changes in the macrocosm – from birth, through mature age, death, and resurrection of the spirit. Darkness is also connected with the concept of the unconscious and the unknown – and so the exploration of this element is linked to the human path to divinity – the lost wholeness. For this reason Naamah is sometimes called "Sleeping" – as she signifies the dark, hidden, and unexplored element in man - the element of darkness that exists in the heart of creation, remaining hidden as a treasure, awaiting to be discovered by a courageous seeker.

Naamah is also the queen of vampires and werewolves, appearing to her followers in the company of ghouls and shades of the dead at burial grounds. In an esoteric sense, this refers to the death principle – and in a deeper meaning – to separation and change. Death is the lord of changes, and thus, the perfect freedom and transformation. However, the ancients viewed the place of death and rest of man, i.e. the grave, as a literal gate to the other side of the world. This is also the function ascribed to the first Qlipha on the Tree of Night ruled by Naamah. The Lilith Qlipha – the womb of the night – is the gate through which the magician enters the other side of creation, facing dark energies and subtle planes of the universe. In this symbolic sense the grave becomes the womb.

This level is also connected with the Muladhara chakra. On the one hand, it is the gate to subtle energies existing in man, as is it suggested by Robert Bruce. Before it is opened, the energy which is gained from the element of earth does not flow freely through other, higher chakras. In the first energy zone the Kundalini serpent lies coiled three and a half times at the base of the spine. Once more this explains the meaning of the name "Sleeping," referring to the unlimited source and potential of sexual energy, which at this level is expressed through basic instincts and urges. Unexplored by the uninitiated, it remains dormant. As a powerful sexual force it is also associated with succubi and incubi, as it was noted in the previous part of this essay. This is also suggested by the sexual nature of Naamah herself. Here we should refer again to the vampiric aspect of the goddess. The magician can awaken the red serpent by working with the root chakra used to drain the energy from the element of earth. And when we master the energy flow within our bodies, we will be able to connect our seven chakras, which are reflections of macrocosmic energies, with our surrounding and drain the power and the force from the world. The person with a perfect mastery of the chakras and a full control of the Kundalini power might become a god.

Naamah is the goddess who challenges the magician and questions the belief in the material image of reality. She opens consciousness to the kingdom of darkness and endows us with all delights and riches of the world – the beauty which is contained in our mind. She seduces and guides us with her music which awakens the ecstasy of life and leads us astray – to wild mountains, woods, and cemeteries – desolate places where we can hear the call of entities from the other side. Thus, we swear the oath of perfection and eternal pursuit of awakening the Great Red Dragon and divinity within. And when we cross the Womb of the Night and find ourselves on the dark side of the world, the fiery breath of the Dragon will become our light through the utmost recesses of Infinity.

Bibliography and quotations:

* *The Bible*
* *Zohar*

Dead Seas Scrolls
* Robert Graves and Raphael Patai: *Hebrew Myths*

Leviathan – "King over all the Sons of Pride"

Asenath Mason

"May those who curse days curse that day,
those who are ready to rouse Leviathan."
(Job 3:8)

The name of this mythical water serpent derives from Hebrew and means "that which gathers itself into folds" or "that which is drawn out." It appears mostly in Christian sources: The Old Testament (Book of Job, Book of Isaiah, Book of Psalms) and in the apocrypha (Book of Enoch, Book of Esdrash), where it refers to a serpent, dragon, crocodile, whale, or generally – a sea beast. Leviathan is also mentioned in the rabbinical literature and in Gnostic accounts. The Bible presents Leviathan as one of the creations of Yahweh:

"There go the ships, and Leviathan
which thou didst form to sport in it." (Psalms 104:26)

Yahweh created this marvelous sea serpent as a pride of the world. Leviathan is, however, also an enemy of Yahweh. He is the embodiment of evil, conceit, darkness and chaos, which this god is continuously striving to defeat. As a seven-headed serpent, Leviathan is one of the Devil's shapes:

"In that day the Lord with his hard and great and strong
sword will punish Leviathan the fleeing serpent,
Leviathan the twisting serpent,
and he will slay the dragon that is in the sea." (Isaiah 27:1)

The Old Testament describes Leviathan as the most
dangerous monster whom Yahweh has to confront. But the
apocrypha and the rabbinical literature mention two
monsters: a male and a female. The female is Leviathan, the
male: Behemoth (plural of "behamah" = "beast").
According to the Midrash, there were two Leviathans
created on the fifth day of Creation. In the beginning, they
were a mated couple, but God, fearing that their offspring
would destroy the world, slew the female monster. Her
flesh will be served up as a dainty to the pious on the Day
of Judgment. The male monster dwells in the seas, in the
Mediterranean Sea in particular, and the waters of Jordan
run into his jaws. His body is 300 miles long, and when he
is hungry, the heat from his mouth causes all waters to boil.
Also, the eyes of Leviathan shine with an odd light, and are
"like the eyelids of the dawn." (Job 41:18).

However, according to the Book of Enoch, Leviathan and
Behemoth will be separated no earlier than on the Day of
Judgment:

"In that day shall be distributed for food two monsters; a
female monster, whose name is Leviathan, dwelling in the
depths of the sea, above the springs of waters; And a male
monster, whose name is Behemoth; which possesses,
moving on his breast, the invisible wilderness. His name
was Dendayen in the east of the garden, where the elect
and the righteous will dwell." (Enoch 7-9)

Then, both monsters will be defeated and Leviathan will be
slain, and his body will be served at the feast of the
righteous. From Leviathan's skin God will make tents for

the most pious people, belts, necklaces and jewelry. The remains of the skin will be hung on the walls of Jerusalem and it will shine on the whole world. According to the legend, it will be Gabriel who will face Leviathan in a fight. But he will not be able to defeat the sea serpent on his own. Neither Yahweh nor any of his angels is powerful enough to slay the beast of the sea. God will command Leviathan and Behemoth (the mountain ox) to enter a duel, and their fight will end with the death of both monsters.

The Judgment Day is similarly presented in the Syriac Apocalypse of Baruch. According to this apocryphal account, Leviathan and Behemoth will be slain on the day of the coming of Messiah, and their flesh will serve as a feast for the chosen.

Another apocryphal work, the so called Books of Esdras, does not foresee Leviathan's and Behemoth's fate. However, it describes them as two monsters that were created on the fifth day and separated because the waters could not hold them together. And so Behemoth went to dwell in the mountains and in the deserts, while for Leviathan God assigned the seventh part of the earth – the one filled with waters. Behemoth became the lord of the dry land, Leviathan – the ruler of waters and all watery creatures.

The description of Leviathan's appearance is given in the Book of Job where he is identified as a crocodile. His back is made of rows of shields. Out of his mouth go flaming torches and sparks of fire leap forth. Out of his nostrils comes forth smoke and his breath can kindle coals. His heart is hard as a stone. When he raises himself up, the mighty are afraid and faint. When he moves, he leaves a shining wake behind. His breath stirs the sea waves. He is the lord of tempests and storms. No weapon can hurt him. He is undefeatable and fears nothing:

"Upon earth there is not his like,
a creature without fear.
He beholds everything that is high;
he is king over all the sons of pride." (Job 41,33-34)

Leviathan and Behemoth appear also in Gnostic sources. The Ophites regarded these two creatures as two (of the seven or ten) circles or stations which the soul has to pass in order to be purged and to attain bliss. In their writings, Leviathan is the soul of the world identified with the Ouroboros serpent.

These two primordial beasts also have many counterparts in other mythologies and legends of different cultures. They are often identified with the Babylonian chaos dragon Tiamat and her consort, Kingu (similarity in the phonetics of Aramaic "akna" = "serpent"). The name "Tiamat" means "abyss," which corresponds to the Hebrew "tehom" – "depths." In the Ugaritic mythology the counterpart of Leviathan is Lotan, identified with another sea deity, Yamm. The biblical story may be based on the Canaanite story of the fight between Yamm and Baal: At the dawn of time there were only two creatures: Yamm and Baal. Yamm, known also as "The Prince of the Seas," was described as a sea monster – dragon, serpent, or seven-headed beast. Baal was the god of storms, clouds and air. These two primordial creatures engaged in a battle for the sovereignty over the world. It ended with Baal's victory over the sea-serpent Yamm.

A similar story is the myth about the fight between the Babylonian god Marduk and the goddess Tiamat, portrayed as a sea dragon and personification of all waters. Out of her flesh he created the earth and human bodies. Leviathan also shares many qualities with other serpents and sea beasts from many other mythologies, e.g. the Scandinavian Jormungandr, Rahab, or Tannin – the sea demons from Jewish legends, the Norwegian Kraken, or the legendary Hydra. Bernard Heuvelmans writes in his book *In the Wake of the Sea-Serpents* that Leviathan could be an authentic giant sea serpent that was seen by many sailors during their sea voyages.

Leviathan
Gustave Doré, XIX century

In the Christian tradition, Leviathan is often identified with Satan, or presented as one of the fallen angels who serve him: the lord of waters and the direction of west. In this form he appears in the grimoire entitled *The Book of the Sacred Magic of Abra-Melin the Mage*. There he is mentioned as one of the main rulers of Hell, together with Lucifer, Belial and Satan. In this aspect he is identified with the angel Rahab, often described as an angel of death. This view also derives from the ancient belief in the relation between the sea beast and darkness, evil – the common attributes of the Devil:

"...Shaitan was being called 'the Old Serpent (dragon)' and 'the Lord of the Abyss.' The Old Serpent or Old Dragon is, according to experts such as E.A. Budge and S.N. Kramer, Leviathan. Leviathan is Lotan. Lotan traces to Tietan. Tietan, we are told by the authorities on Near Eastern mythology is a Later form of Tiamat. According to the experts the Dragon of the Abyss called Shaitan is the same Dragon of the Abyss named Tiamat." (2)

Leviathan is also described as an intermediary between Lilith and Satan-Samael, the pair of hellish rulers. Moreover – he is the image of their union: "You already know that evil Samael and wicked Lilith are like a sexual pair who, by means of an intermediary, receive an evil and wicked emanation from one and emanate to the other. I shall explain this relying on the esoteric meaning in the verse 'In that day the Lord will punish with His great, cruel, mighty sword Leviathan the twisted serpent and Leviathan the tortuous serpent' - this is Lilith – 'and He will slay the dragon of the sea' (Isaiah 27:1). As there is a pure Leviathan in the sea and it is called a serpent, so there is a great defiled serpent in the sea in the literal sense. The same holds true above in a hidden way. The heavenly serpent is a blind prince, the image of an intermediary between Samael and Lilith. Its name is Tanin'iver... He is the bond, the accompaniment, and the union between Samael and Lilith. If he were created whole in the fullness of his emanation he would have destroyed the world in an instant." (4)

For this reason the name Leviathan (LvTHN) appears on the symbol of Baphomet, a representation of the union between Lilith and Samael, as an encircling and eternal force – the symbol taken by Anton LaVey from the French occultist Eliphas Levi.

In the medieval encyclopedia of biblical art, the so-called *Liber Floridus*, we can see Leviathan as a beast carrying on its back the Antichrist. Leviathan is presented here as a beast resembling a dragon, with black eyes and sharp teeth. The drawing implies that the Antichrist draws his force from the beast he is riding. This is confirmed by the Apocalypse of St. John: "Men worshipped the dragon, for he had given his authority to the beast." (Revelation 13:4)

Symbolically, Leviathan represents most of all the lower forces, the primeval chaos that creates the balance in the cosmic order. He is also the primordial beast serving as a cosmogonic sacrifice – as Marduk defeats Tiamat, or Baal slays Yamm, so Yahweh kills the female Leviathan and uses her skin and flesh as elements of other creations. The "garments of light" prepared for Adam and Eve were created from the skin of the slain Leviathan. Because "garments" are interpreted as flesh covering human soul, thus the bodies of humans are a part of the primordial chaos beast.

Michael Aquino writes in *The Diabolicon*: "Before God or Angel, Daemon or man, there was Leviathan alone, principle of continuity and ageless existence." Leviathan represents therefore the very beginning, the original cosmic force that gave rise to the universe. Not accidentally, the Gnostics believed that he is the Anima Mundi, the soul of the world. He is the eternal beginning and ending. He cannot be defeated or tamed because the slain dragon/serpent always rises back to life, or exists as a part of the world and humanity. One can awaken and summon him, which is told by Job who curses the night of his own birth and says that there are people skillful to do it. In the microcosmic sense, Leviathan represents the darkest levels of the unconscious. He is the element of chaos and the potential of the force lying dormant in the dark recesses of the human psyche.

Leviathan is what binds the astral and the physical bodies. He represents self-control and mastering of the self through a dynamic change. He is both the above and the below – the inner and the outer force, the soul of the world and the divine spark. He is the timeless existence, the principle that wakes and binds the essence of the self. You can find him by immersing yourself in the depths of the unconscious, in dreams and visions through which the impulses of the unknown are brought to the light of consciousness. This process is an integral part of the left hand path, where the adept gradually reaches the center of consciousness by immersion in its inner core – in search for potential that enables one to shape reality – both the inner and the outer. Through walking the path of Leviathan we become as him – the Serpent/Dragon, the divine being, separate from all cosmic structures. All we have to strive for is to become aware of and master the spark of divinity, the essence of Leviathan.

Bibliography:

1) Kaufmann Kohler, W.H. Bennet, Louis Ginzberg: *The Jewish Encyclopedia*
2) Ryan Parker: *Necronomicon Info Source*
3) The Bible
4) R. Isaac b. Jacob Ha-Kohen: *Treatise on the Left Emanation*
5) Michael Aquino: *The Diabolicon*
6) Manfred Lurker: *Lexicon of Gods and Demons*

Invocation of Leviathan

Asenath Mason

If possible, perform the ritual outside, near the sea or the ocean. In other cases, put the image of Leviathan on your altar and burn the incense related to the scents of the seaside. Pour salty water into your chalice and place it on the altar as well.

I invoke Leviathan! Lord of the Waters! Dragon of the Sea who is the gate to the depths of my soul! Awaken from your slumber and rise up from the abyss to open the door to forgotten knowledge!

LEPACA KLIFFOTH!

Envision yourself standing on the shore of a great sea. It is night and everything is dark. The only thing you can see is the sky full of bright stars. The sea is calm and it is chilly.

I invoke you, creature of the fifth day of Creation; the great Dragon who makes seas alive.
You are the leader of all the watery realms.
Your power is unlimited and your 300 eyes shine in the dark like the eyelids of the dawn.
Out of your mouth go flaming torches and sparks of fire leap forth.
Out of your nostrils comes forth smoke, and a flame comes forth from your mighty jaws!

HO DRAKON HO MEGAS!

I summon you, immortal and infinite god!
Lord of waters, the primeval substance out of which all life emerged.
Arise from your sleep and take the rule over the world that is your destiny!
Manifest your power to those who are skillful enough to raise you!
Reveal the hidden sources of ancient wisdom!

VOVIN! VOVIN! LEPACA VOVIN!

Suddenly a wind starts to blow. It gets colder and colder. The sky is covered with clouds. Enormous waves appear on the surface of the sea. The storm begins. Bolts of lightning are striking around you and you can hear thunders and the roaring of the sea. From the water emerges the great Serpent-Dragon. He is black. His scales shine in flashes of lightning. He is surrounded by an aura of electricity. His eyes shine with a phosphoric light. The Serpent swims toward the shore in your direction. Now you are standing opposite him and facing his magnetic eyes.

And the time of awakening has come!
The seas part and give birth to great beasts under the leadership of the Great Dragon!
A new age begins – the aeon of Leviathan rising!

At this moment the storm calms down. Clouds move away and the sky full of stars appears again. The wind ceases to blow. You feel energy flowing toward you from the Serpent's eyes. You cannot take your eyes away from him. You are no longer cold. A feeling of calmness overwhelms you.

The Serpent awakens!
The Dragon stretches his wings and his shadow covers the
earth.
The old gods rise from the oceans!
Arise in me, Leviathan!

I hail you!
Ho Drakon Ho Megas!

Suddenly the Serpent leans over you, opens his mouth and devours you. Now you are in his stomach. You feel warmth which slowly turns into heat. The fire starts to burn in your body. It rises at the base of the spine and flows upward, embracing the whole body. Your breath pulsates in the same rhythm as the breath of the Serpent.

Your body is transforming. Your skin turns to scales. Wings grow from your back. You are surrounded by an electric aura. Now you are the Serpent-Dragon. Seas and oceans are your kingdom. You feel an enormous force flowing inside you. You can raise and stop winds, incite storm and stir the sea. You are the lord of the watery abyss. Your body is inflamed with a force unknown to humans. You feel unity of all elements. You are the union of heaven and earth, air and fire, water and earth. Meditate upon this feeling and absorb all that comes to you with this experience.

The Living Death: Two Faces of the Feminine: Lilith and Az (Jeh)

Pairika-Eva Borowska

"After Ohrmazd had given women to righteous men, they fled and went over a Satan; and when Ohrmazd provided righteous men with peace and happiness, Satan provided women too with happiness. As Satan had allowed the women to ask for anything they wanted, Ohrmazd feared that they might ask to have intercourse with the righteous men and that these might suffer damage thereby."

(Theodore bar Konai)

Legends about Lilith derive mostly from Assyrian-Babylonian and Hebrew traditions. This vampiric goddess of the night has a great significance also in the Qabalah and Talmudic demonology, and as a goddess of the underground current, she influenced the origins of the Qabalah in Saracen Spain. We know that Lilith is believed to appear in the Book of Isaiah [34,14] and the Book of Job [18,15]. Apart from these short mentions, nothing else can be found in today's Bible. We also know that Lilith was the first wife of Adam, the first rebel and the herald of the conscious Free Will. In myths about Lilith we find stories in which Adam first felt envy while watching animals copulate, and asked God for a female companion. Thus, God created Lilith – a being similar to Adam, but made of ash, mud and filth. United with Adam, Lilith gave birth to many demons which later were to torment mankind. Their relationship was not perfect, though. Lilith dared to oppose Adam and questioned his superiority, especially in their sexual relations. She did not agree to take the passive role in the intercourse and often asked:

"Why do I always have to lie beneath? I am your equal."

But Adam could not understand her demands, did not want to listen to her, and most of all, did not want to give her what she desired. Instead, he spoke to her about God's law that a woman must be obedient to her husband. Then Lilith, infuriated, screamed the unspeakable name of God (Shem Hamforash), spread her wings, and fled from Eden to a wilderness near the Red Sea. There, in the land of Zemargad, she created her own "garden of pleasures." The Garden of Eden was for her nothing more than a prison without the right to liberty and equality, ruled by the patriarchal principle. This was not what she desired.

Lilith was the first to long for free choice, Free Will. When she left the Garden of Eden, for the first time she had a chance to taste both Darkness and Light. In her kingdom on the shores of the Red Sea she gave birth to thousands of demons, over a hundred each day. Her children were called Lilitu or Lilim, and it is sometimes said that their number was 784, which is the Qabalistic number of Lilith. After she left, Adam complained to God that his companion fled from him, and God sent three angels, Senoy, Sansenoy and Semangelof, to bring her back. Yet, she did not want to exchange her newly gained freedom for imprisonment in the patriarchal structure, and she refused to return, for which she was punished: each day a hundred of her demons were to die. Angry at this judgment, Lilith swore vengeance upon God's beloved creation: man. Thus, whenever she had a chance, she devoured the offspring of man, especially male infants.

Lilith personifies the dark side of the feminine: rebellious and untamed nature, eroticism and debauchery, desire, passion and viciousness. It is her who haunts men in their darkest dreams, sending them visions of lechery and forbidden satisfaction, and steals their semen so that she can use it to create more succubi and incubi. She is therefore a symbol of sexual delights, but also she signifies the fear of impotence and weakness (for how man can be weaker from his wife?). On the Tree of Night, as the dark queen, Lilith is the ruler of the second Qlipha, Gamaliel, while her name is ascribed to another Qliphothic sphere: Malkuth/Lilith, ruled by Naamah/Nahemah, which means "pleasant," while the name "Lilith" might be translated as "screeching" or "li-lit" – "evil spirit" (among other meanings). The level of Malkuth, also called "the womb of Lilith," represents the absorption of energies essential to walk the initiatory path through the Tree of Night in order to find self-deification. There we find the goddess in her lair, in the caves and pits of the earth, in the lakes of her nourishing blood. Naamah is known as the demon of prostitution and a demonic sister to Lilith, or a sister to Tubal Cain. As the legend has it, from the union of Adam (possessed by Samael) and Eve (possessed by Lilith) Cain was born, the first murderer and the father to the Cainites. He was the first man who achieved higher gnosis after being taught the secrets of the universe by his true mother, Lilith. Her vampiric nature is also represented by an insatiable hunger, both in the sense of life and sexual gratification, and her connection to the lunar cycle of the woman. As the mistress of the dark side of the moon, the mythical lair of vampires, she is life and death conjoined, the personification of the united principles of Eros and Thanatos. Lilith is also the mother and the ruler of the Sabbat, where through ecstasy, dark and savage sexual practices, she represents primeval and natural instincts of man and the mysteries of witchcraft. She has hundreds of names which can be used to call her. According to a legend, she revealed seventeen of them to the prophet Elias. Some of them were: Abeko, Abito, Amizo, Batna, Izorpo, Kali, Kea, Kokos, Odam, Lilith, Patrota, Podo, Satrina, Talto.

According to some legends, after Abel's death Adam refrained from sexual intercourse with Eve, but instead he fornicated with Lilith. The offspring of this union was reputedly a wise frog. The frog taught mankind languages and the knowledge of herbs and gems. But the Church rejects these legends as the frog is considered an impure animal, of the Devil's origin. Here we should mention the old Iranian myths where the frog is one of the forms of Ahriman, the devil of these religions. Ahriman's consort is Jeh, also known as Az, a demon akin to Lilith. Unfortunately, there are not many sources on Az, but what we can actually find, reveals her as a very interesting entity. The name "Jeh" itself, which derives from the Pahlavi texts, means "whore," or "harlot." Thus, she is known as "The Whore of Whores" or "The Queen of Whores," the one who will awaken mankind to sin, debauchery and sexual pleasures. In Ahrimanic myths, Az has a significant role – she is his inspiration and force arousing his desires. Also, she was the one who awakened Ahriman from his three-thousand-year sleep, to which he was put by his righteous brother Ahura Mazda. Jeh can be viewed as an equivalent of such goddesses/female demons as Lilith or Babalon, the Whore. She is most often depicted as a beautiful woman, a fly, a dragon, or as a disgusting crone. Her lair is in the places untouched by the rays of sun, in caves or in the darkest of hells. She was the one who taught humans, demons, the daevas, and later the fallen angels how to arouse oneself and others, how to copulate and fornicate. Az is the first woman who used witchcraft to create dragon children, demons and daughters, who were the only creatures from her blood. Similarly as Lilith, she was known to devour her offspring and their progeny, after which she gave birth to more children which also devoured one another in the eternal cycle. Az is viewed as the instinctual side of man, based on basic urges: dying and living, eating and copulating. Therefore Zaehner regards her as the instinctual aspect of each human, the unrestrained movement which is anticlockwise, antinomian and chaotic.

"The demon Az is a Buddhist rather than a Zoroastrian idea; there is no trace of it in the Avesta. In Buddhism, on the other hand, the root cause of the chain of conditioned existence is *avidya*, 'ignorance,' and its principal manifestation is *trshna*, 'thirst,' which means the desire for continued existence in time - intellectual error, then, manifesting itself in concupiscence."

In the Zoroastrian religion Az represents the concept of deification through the conscious dedication of oneself to the path of sexual debauchery and predatory vampirism. Thus, Az and Lilith both stand for the Left Hand Path as a transition from light into darkness through the process of becoming a whole among chaos and non-being. The union of Ahriman and Az is connected to the three-thousand-year fall of Satan, punished by Ahura Mazda, the god of light. Unconscious Satan had not been awakened by his servants – demons and shadows - through their stories of fighting and heroic deeds, until Az came to him and said:

"Arise, O our father, for in the battle [to come] I shall let loose so much affliction on the Righteous Man and the toiling Bull that, because of my deeds, they will no be fit to live. I shall take away their dignity (*khwarr*): I shall afflict the water, I shall afflict the earth, I shall afflict the fire, I shall afflict the plants, I shall afflict all the creation which Ohrmazd has created."

After hearing these words, Ahriman awakened from his infinite slumber and rose, ready to fight. Zaehner mentions such a description of his awakening and his gift to Az:

"And she related her evil deeds so minutely that the Destructive Spirit was comforted, leapt up out of his swoon, and kissed the head of the Whore; and that pollution called menstruation appeared on the Whore. And the Destructive Spirit cried out to the demon Whore: 'Whatsoever is thy desire, that do thou ask, that I may give it thee.'"

In the Bundahishn we may find a similar description of the "kiss," which obviously stands for sexual intercourse:

"And he kissed Jeh upon the head, and the pollution which they call menstruation became apparent in Jeh."

From all this we can draw two main conclusions. First of all, Az or Jeh possesses the knowledge of Light and Darkness, of the Natural Order, the knowledge which is not possessed by Ahriman. Az might have been therefore created with the same knowledge as possessed by Zurvan, the father of Ahura Mazda (the god of light) and Ahriman (the god of darkness). Thus, she is a woman who knows all of life and death and is able to teach the ways of self-deification and self-creation. She is more intelligent and wiser than the male element. She evokes respect, fear, lust and passions. The other thing which is worth to note is that Jeh, who was endowed with menstrual blood and viewed as impure, personifies the dark side of the moon, the vampire concept. Moon and menstrual blood are symbolic of a certain natural cycle. It belongs to the lunar sphere, which in the Western esotericism is called the astral plane, the realm of vampirism and the place of the spiritual Sabbat.

To sum up, Az and Lilith are the goddesses of the astral realm, where the magician can participate in debauched Sabbats, wild celebrations of freedom and lust. Through this desire and gratification on sexual and spiritual levels, one can enter the path of self-creation and self-perfection, as through the Sabbatic union we may experience all our hidden instincts, essential to the full integration of consciousness. Lilith and Az represent the night, the storm, sex, lust, passion, and also life and death. As a female principle, more perfect than male, and as those who were the first to experience and possess full knowledge of the universe, they have never been and never will be slaves of any god or man. They are the archetype of Femme Fatale, the vampiric seductress and the one who awakens the dead to life. They are the mistresses of the Blood-Red Moon and patronesses of witches. They are the ever-changing female principle. What is really significant to notice is that both of them are aware of their power and potential, and the release of these forces is viewed as a threat to social structures and religions of the patriarchal world.

Bibliography:

1. Piotr Piotrowski: *Lilith Czarny Księżyc*
2. Michael W. Ford: *Aryman - perski diabeł i Nierządnica Ciemności*
3. Retorius: *Sabat w ujęciu perskim*
4. Michael W. Ford: *Yatuk Dinoih*
5. Michael W. Ford *Book of the Witch Moon*
6. Michael W. Ford: *Book of Cain*
7. Asenath Mason: *Lilith – Pani ciemnej strony ludzkiej natury*
8. B. Black Koltuv: *The Book of Lilith*

Invocation to Az

Pairika-Eva Borowska

*Oh Az, give me the power and strength to create, to
destroy, and to annihilate the dualisms of this world!
To walk the path of self-deification!
Az, Lady of the Desert Nights,
I offer you my body in humiliation and in beauty!
Whore of Whores,
Mother of demonic spawn and the creatures of the night,
I summon you!
You, who awoke Ahriman from his eternal sleep,
I call you by your names:*

AZ! JEH! KALI! LILITH! HEKATE! BABALON! TIAMAT!

*Az, Goddess of Darkness, Debauchery, Wisdom and
Witchcraft,
You possess the powers to summon and bind,
You awaken the dead to life,
Az – Jeh, tasting the blood of your own children,
Give me the power of self-creation!*

Meditation upon the Congress with Az

Pairika-Eva Borowska

Envision that you are in a hot desert. Around, you can see nothing more than dry sand and the blood-red sun which scorches your skin. Your senses are burnt by the tormenting fire of the wilderness. You walk for such a long time that you can feel you are scorched to death by the ruthless sun.

In the distance you suddenly notice black caves emerging from the landscape of golden and red desert sand. You think this is an illusion but you go in this direction. As you come closer, you are aware that the caves are real and they seem inviting with their refreshing coolness.

The mistress of this cold lair is Az, whom you meet inside and whom you should greet with the words: "Lepaca Kliffoth." She gives you a chalice filled with her menstrual blood which tastes like the most wonderful nectar. You sink into the abyss of darkness of your own mind, in search for the knowledge of self-deification. Az will be your guide on this journey. She will reveal to you her symbol by which you will be able to summon her next time, without the need to cross the desert.

When you wish to summon her again, draw the glyph on the sand and open yourself for the contact with the goddess. In return for knowledge, Az may demand your body. Give yourself to her without hesitation then. Remember, she hates the weak and the doubtful! Upon leaving, give her your thanks and greet her with the words: "Ho Drakon Ho Megas."

The Serpent - Ancient Guardian of Wisdom

Asenath Mason

Serpents were worshipped as sacred animals from time immemorial. Ancient people associated them with divine spheres and ascribed many mystical attributes to these chthonic creatures. Serpents were identified with many phenomena and their symbolism is very complex. The mystical qualities of this animal were usually connected with one dominant feature, e.g. crawling, skin-removal, shape, deadly venom, etc. No less significant were the characteristics connected with places where serpents dwelt, such as forests, deserts, seas, lakes, water vessels, and other locations. The snake was a symbol of destruction as well as an emblem of life and fertility. It was connected with the feminine element, but it was also a phallic symbol, the biblical snake-tempter who led humans to sin, or a savior – the bearer of knowledge and wisdom. Many ancient gods and entities were depicted as serpents. Snakes were also associated with a variety of natural forces – this symbol had an enormous influence which has not declined even in the modern world.

The symbolism of the serpent is connected in a mystical way with the feminine principle. The serpent which dwells in the chthonic regions is in a continual union with Mother Earth – the personified maternity. The earth for ages has been perceived as the Great Mother, the one who gives birth, feeds, and nourishes, the source of all life and fertility. The connection between the serpent and the earth element indicated its female aspect, the principle of fertility, maternity, and femininity. However, the female element does not only refer to fertility and maternity but also to all that is mysterious, unforeseen, intuitive, irrational. The biblical Serpent turns to Eve, not to Adam. Eve's rival, demonic Lilith, is also often identified with the serpent. Many ancient goddesses were depicted as women holding serpents in their hands. Among them we can find such mythological characters as Hecate, Persephone, and Artemis. The ancient Egyptian goddess of fertility was called Renenutet and was depicted as a half-serpent half-woman. Her name meant "renen" - "food" and "utet" – "serpent." In ancient Greece she was known as Thermutis.[1] There are also mythological characters depicted with snakes instead of hair, like the Erinyes, Gorgon, or Echidna, the demonic snake-woman from Greek mythology. In central Europe, there was a common belief that if you bury a woman's hair under the moonlight, they will turn into serpents.[2] Nevertheless, the serpent was also a phallic symbol, an impregnating masculine force connected with sun rays or bolts of lightning. In this context, the masculine or the feminine role of the serpent as a symbol is highly ambivalent.

Goddesses associated with serpents were not only deities of the earth but also of the underworld, the darkness and the black cosmic womb. Ancient Greeks believed that the soul of a dead person assumes the shape of a serpent. That is why the serpent was often considered as a chthonic symbol, the personified power of the underworld, dark otherworldly forces, and the primordial energy of cosmic darkness. In this aspect the serpent was a symbol of the

---

[1] Manfred Lurker: *Dictionary of Gods and Goddesses, Devils and Demons*

[2] Juan Cirlot: *Dictionary of Symbols*

dark side of human nature, the principle hidden in the unconscious. In the Qabalah, Qliphothic levels of the Tree of Night are considered to be a domain of forces depicted as serpents or dragons. The Egyptian god Apophis, the snake-demon that threatens the Sun God's daily journey through the underworld, can be a proper example. Ra has to fight Apophis every day during his passage through Amenti. Egyptian myths describe how the demonic serpent is killed by the sun god and his blood dyes the skies red at dawn. Apophis is sometimes identified with Set or the demonic Typhon – the dragon-headed and serpent-legged monster. Other demonic serpents appearing in the world's mythologies are e.g. Leviathan, Jormungandr, or Vritra. Ahriman, the Persian personification of evil, appears in depictions with the head of a lion and a serpent coiled around his body. However, not only the fearsome, demonic entities were associated with serpents. The snake was also the attribute of benevolent deities. Atum – the ancient Egyptian creator of the world – was sometimes depicted as a serpent. Serpents also appear as the attribute of Athena. Varuna, the highest god of the Vedic religion, bears the name of "Nagaraja," "King of Serpents." In the Hindu beliefs, the Naga serpents are demonic entities, often depicted as half-humans, half-snakes, with five or seven heads. Their role and qualities are not entirely negative. The Ananta serpent is the symbol of Infinity. Sesha uplifts the Earth. Vasuki acts as a rope which stirs the sea and frightens other demons away for Shiva. In the Hindu folklore the Naga serpents are worshipped as patrons of fertility. In Tibet they are regarded as benevolent water deities who watch over the Buddhist writings.[3]

It is also worth noticing that deities, spirits and demons depicted as serpents were often connected with water. This

---

[3] Manfred Lurker: *Dictionary of Gods and Goddesses, Devils and Demons*

view owes much to the symbolism of the female aspect in which the water element has always played a pivotal role. Leviathan, Jormungandr, as well as other serpent entities were often water creatures. This also refers to deities depicted as dragons, like the Babylonian dragon-goddess Tiamat (embodying the concept of salty waters) and Apsu (fresh waters). The connection between serpents, dragons and water was the result of their primordial, chaotic nature. The primordial chaos was often described as ancient waters from which the whole universe was born. The serpent-like nature of the ancient gods implies therefore their connection to the primordial energy, the principle of chaos, being the source of creative potential. This is highly evocative of the Kundalini energy which represents the internal psychic force in the tradition of Tantrism. We also find its equivalent in other world cultures. The Egyptian uraeus is a symbol of transformation by ascension, similar to the process of Kundalini awakening when it ascends through seven traditional energy levels, the chakras. Similar motifs are found in ancient Mesopotamia – the ascent through the levels of the ziggurat, or the way through steps made of seven metals in rituals of Mithras. Kundalini is the force which awakens and transforms consciousness, leading to spiritual initiation and rebirth of senses.

The ascent of the Kundalini serpent also indicates the serpent's role as the mediator between the worlds – the lower and the higher, the earth and the heavens, or the earth and the underworld. The best known example of this concept is the Caduceus, two snakes coiled around the staff crowned with a pair of wings. This symbol has been known from ancient times. In ancient Rome it represented the spiritual and moral balance. The staff denoted power, serpents – wisdom, and wings – diligence. The Caduceus can be successfully compared to Tantric ideas about Kundalini as the emblem of the transformative energy of human evolution. This energy is symbolized by ascending serpents. Coiled around the staff, which represents the axis of the universe, the serpents embody the concept of a precise, mutual symmetry, the active balance of opposite forces. They stand for the earth, the lower forces, the earthly instincts, and the underworld. The pair of wings on top of the Caduceus is the higher world, the symbol of the Spirit. The Caduceus was also the attribute of Hermes/Mercury – the messenger of the gods and mediator between the worlds. Hermes is the psychopomp who guides souls from the worldly life into the great beyond, leads them from the world of humans to the Other Side. Alchemy attributes to this deity one of the most important functions in the process of transmutation. The alchemical Mercury represents the unconscious liquid and dynamic energy that has a double nature – feminine and masculine, higher and lower. It is the symbol of *complexio oppositorum*. His other names are *Monstrum Hermaphroditus* or *Rebis*. In alchemy, it is the agent of transformation, endowed with a huge creative potential, inseparably connected with other concepts of the serpent. Mercury's Caduceus is also a symbol of polarization of opposites, integration of elements: staff - earth, wings - air, serpents – water and fire. The Greek myth about the prophet Tiresias, who was transformed into a woman after he had separated two copulating snakes (the Caduceus) and into a man again after he did the same seven years later, shows that the serpent was considered to be closely connected with the transformation of opposites. These serpents, as well as those coiling around the Caduceus, are Ida and Pingala from the Hindu tradition. Kundalini unites the opposite elements: earth with air through its journey upward, and water, the feminine element - when it flows through the left nadi (Ida) with the masculine element of fire – when it flows through the right nadi (Pingala). In the last stage of the journey occurs the synthesis of the opposites – the serpent becomes the dragon – the winged embodiment of the Quintessence.

Adam and Eve in Paradise
From *The Children's Bible Picture Book*, 1875

Many traditions depict the dragon as a winged serpent. Medieval dragons had the chest and feet of an eagle, the body of a serpent, the wings of a bat, and the tail ending with a pointed spike. Each of these elements represented a distinct quality: the eagle – the heavenly aspect, the serpent – the mystery and the underworld, the wings – the intellect, the tail – the reason. This is, however, only one of numerous interpretations of the dragon symbol. Like the serpent, the dragon was the mediator between the worlds, embodying particular aspects of the universe and all elements existing in nature. Cirlot observes that both the dragon and the serpent personify the rhythm of life in the whole universe, which is particularly easy to notice on the example of the Chinese tradition:

"The association of dragon/lightning/rain/fecundity is very common in archaic Chinese texts, for which reason the fabulous animal becomes the connecting link between the Upper Waters and earth. However, it is impossible to generalize about the dragon from the Chinese mythology, for there are subterranean, aerial and aquatic dragons. 'The earth joins up with the dragon' means that it is raining. It plays an important part as an intermediary, then, between the two extremes of the cosmic forces associated with the essential characteristics of the three-level symbolism, that is: the highest level of spirituality; the intermediary plane of the phenomenal life; and the lower level of inferior and telluric forces."[4]

Serpents coiling around the Caduceus also resemble an image of a serpent coiling around a tree, which is common for many cultures worldwide. Like the Caduceus staff, the tree symbolizes the *axis mundi*, the axis connecting particular levels and dimensions of the whole universe – the lower worlds (the underworld, hell) are the roots of the tree, while the higher, heavenly planes are symbolized by leaves and branches. The trunk is the axis through which the soul can travel between the worlds. This concept corresponds to Shushumna, the central nadi in Tantrism,

---

[4] Juan Cirlot: *Dictionary of Symbols*

through which the Kundalini serpent makes its ascent. The serpent coiled around a tree is also symbolic of the harmony of cosmic forces. Usually, this image also includes an eagle sitting on top of the tree. In this sense, the serpent is one of the fundamental archetypes in the synthesis of forces that constitute the universe.

In myths and legends the serpent is almost always a wise creature, often depicted as personifying wisdom and power. In ancient Greece, the serpent was sacred to Athena, the goddess of wisdom. In one of the myths she is – in a sense – the mother of the serpent-man Erichtonios who was born from Hephaestus' semen which ejaculated on the ground when Athena resisted him and vanished.[5] In Egypt, the cobra was considered to be the symbol of power and knowledge, the highest wisdom – both divine and royal, the domain of pharaohs, the children of gods. The winged serpent, or a dragon, according to some myths, guards treasures, gems and great riches hidden in mountainous caves. A similar function is sometimes attributed to snakes. The Naga are guardians of temples. It is also the serpent that guards the Tree of Knowledge and the Well of Immortality. These treasures are symbols of knowledge and wisdom which can only be gained by strong and courageous heroes who do not fear to face the danger. In an esoteric sense, the quest for treasures guarded by primordial reptiles is a symbol of initiation. It is a spiritual journey in search for the lost knowledge. The biblical Serpent is the seducer, described as evil incarnate, the Adversary who leads humans to eternal damnation. His role in the Garden of Eden, however, might be interpreted in several different ways. He represents the alternative to salvation through God: the path of independence and self-responsibility. He is the initiator of

---

[5] Manfred Lurker: *Dictionary of Gods and Goddesses, Devils and Demons*

mankind and the emblem of the path toward self-deification. Helena Blavatsky observes that in ancient magical traditions the name "Serpent" or "Dragon" was given to people of knowledge, initiated adepts.[6] The Gnostics believed that the serpent personified the principle of salvation. Eve's temptation to eat the fruits from the Tree of Knowledge was equivalent to liberating humans from the force of cosmic oppression. Many Gnostic doctrines included the cult of the serpent, such as e.g. the Naasseni (from Hebrew *na'ash* – "snake"), or the Ophites (from Greek *ophis*). They claimed that the serpent was the savior of mankind because he taught man the divine secrets and revealed the true knowledge, the gnosis. In *The Gnostic Religion* Hans Jonas describes the Gnostic story of salvation in the following way: the heavenly mother, Sophia-Prunikos decided to destroy the demiurgic work of her malevolent son Ialdabaoth and sent the serpent to tempt Adam and Eve to break Ialdabaoth's commandments. The plan was successful – they both ate the fruits from the forbidden tree. But when they did so, they became aware of forces which existed outside their world and turned away from their creators. This was the first victory of the transcendental principle over the force that blocked man's access to knowledge. Until that time, man was merely the hostage of Light. The serpent's deed marked the beginning of Gnosis on earth.

The Ophites were one of the earliest Gnostic sects, active in the second century in Syria and Egypt. In their doctrine, the serpent symbolized the knowledge allowing for liberation from the shackles of the mundane world. It was the initiator of man's individual path, opposed to the laws of the universe, leading to self-salvation. But also in the Gnostic religions the symbolism of the serpent has a certain ambivalence. There is the Agathodaimon, representing

---

[6] Helena Blavatsky: *The Secret Doctrine*

benevolent qualities, and Kakodaimon, connected with the evil element. The Gnostic serpent is Nous and Logos. He is often associated with the feminine force of Sophia/Ennoia, the One Who Gives Birth to Everything, the *Anima Mundi*. In this sense, the serpent represents the feminine wisdom, intuition, repetition, rhythm, creation. Unlike in the teachings of the Ophites, other Gnostic doctrines included the serpent's connection to the primordial darkness, cosmic abyss, and dark waters. He was not only the savior but also the ruler and the essence of evil existing in the world. The gigantic snake/dragon was thought to coil around the globe, encircling the earth in its eternal embrace. The Gnostic treatise *Pistis Sophia* claims: "In the outer darkness there is a great dragon having its tail in its mouth."[7] This serpent is an archaic symbol, most often referred to as Ouroboros. This motif appears in many cultures, in Egypt, Greece, etc., not only as the Gnostic symbol. Ouroboros has a very complex meaning. He represents the time and the *continuum* of life, cyclic changes in nature, death and rebirth. His images sometimes include the inscription "En to pan" (One is All). The serpent devouring his own tail stands for eternal movement. Ouroboros kills himself, marries himself, impregnates himself, devours himself, and gives birth to himself – this is the union of opposites and the primordial self-sufficiency. He can be interpreted as the union of male and female elements because half of his body is bright and the other half dark. It implies the union of opposing principles, like in the Chinese Yin-Yang symbol in which Yang represents masculine force and Yin - feminine. Ouroboros is therefore another example of a variety of meanings attributed to the symbolism of the serpent and its connection to extremes: the positive and the negative. He represents the primordial state of existence that contains both darkness and light, destruction and

---

[7] Hans Jonas: *The Gnostic Religion*

creative potential. This is the archetypal darkness in human consciousness.

We can also find the motif of the cosmic serpent coiling around the globe in the Vodou tradition. Here he is called Damballah and depicted as a serpent leaned over the path through which the sun walks each day. Sometimes he is united with his female counterpart, Aida, the rainbow. Damballah is the patron of the heavenly waters and springs and rivers on the earthly plane. When he hides in the sea, the cosmic waters reflect him as the rainbow. Damballah and Aida form a sexual union. They both encircle the cosmos, like the serpent coiled around the whole universe.[8]

Ouroboros crawls through each location and each element, connecting the world in a cosmic harmony. The Ophites believed that the serpent lives in every single object and in every single creature. Their doctrine recognized seven circles, levels corresponding to the structure of the universe. This is reminiscent of the Tantric concept of the Kundalini serpent which ascends upward through seven chakras. The chakras represent the levels of the ascent toward the Divine, like the Mesopotamian ziggurats which had seven terraces dedicated to particular gods, symbolizing the structure of the universe. Seven is the number often mentioned in association with the serpent or the dragon. In myths and legends we often encounter seven-headed snakes and dragons. Almost all dragons from ancient mythologies had seven heads. According to Blavatsky, seven heads symbolize the seven elements that the nature and human beings consist of. The seventh, central head, is the most important.[9] In certain esoteric traditions there are seven levels of energy that constitute

[8] Maya Deren: *Divine Horsemen: The Living Gods of Haiti*
[9] Helena Blavatsky: *The Secret Doctrine*

the world. Their manifestation is reflected in particular aspects of nature: the seven colors of the rainbow, the seven stars of the Great Bear Constellation, the seven directions in the space, the seven planets of traditional astrology, etc. Blavatsky writes:

"The seven Northern constellations make up the Black Warrior; the seven Eastern (Chinese autumn) constitute the White Tiger; the seven Southern are the Vermilion Bird; and the seven Western (called Vernal) are the Azure Dragon. Each of these four Spirits presides over its heptanomis during one lunar week. The genetive of the first heptanomis (Typhon of the Seven Stars) now took a lunar character; in this phase we find the goddess Sefekh, whose name signifies number 7, is the feminine word, or *logos* in place of the mother of Time, who was the earlier *Word*, as goddess of the Seven Stars."[10]

Seven is also the number of days in a week, planetary deities, but also the Christian cardinal sins. It was believed in Bavaria that the seventh son of the same parents becomes a werewolf. Seven was the number of Saturn and his influences, both positive and negative. It had an enormous meaning in occult philosophy. However, there were also dragons with the number of heads different than seven. The three-headed dragon, for instance, symbolizes three essences – the active, the passive and the neutral.[11]

Serpent's venom can be a deadly poison or a mystical elixir which heals and transforms. The serpent coiling around a chalice is the emblem often encountered in medicine and pharmaceuticals. Also, in ancient times the serpent was the attribute of deities that were believed to have healing powers. Asclepius, the Greek god of healing and medical

---

[10] *Ibid.*
[11] Juan Cirlot: *Dictionary of Symbols*

arts, was sometimes depicted as a serpent and probably originally was a serpent deity. In one of his depictions he holds a rod with a snake coiled around. His daughter Hygeia, the goddess of health, is depicted in a similar way. Her sacred animal and companion is the serpent. This also refers to the serpent's skill of rejuvenation through the removal of the skin, which is an old symbol of renovation and resurrection, both in the physical and spiritual senses. This is why the serpent sometimes appears in images holding a fruit or herb of immortality in his jaws.[12]

Serpents and dragons also represent the unconscious instincts, dark and hidden aspects of the human nature. For this reason they often have demonic character. In the human brain there are still parts that we share with our evolutionary ancestors, reptiles and beasts. Peter J. Carroll observes:

"All the dragons, serpents and scaly demons of myth and nightmare are reptile atavisms out of the older parts of our brains. Evolution has not deleted these ancestral behaviour patterns, merely buried them under a pile of new modifications. Thus, in mythology the gods, as representatives of human consciousness, suppress the titans and dragons of the older consciousness."[13]

Serpents symbolize the unconscious forces that have been repressed from our conscious mind. Confrontation with them is often seen as destructive and frightening. Liberation of these instincts means the necessity to face the mystical qualities of the unconscious, traditionally viewed as dark and negative and suppressed by cultures and religions. Myths and legends describe this as the

---

[12] Manfred Lurker: *Dictionary of Gods and Goddesses, Devils and Demons*
[13] Peter J. Carroll: *Liber Null & Psychonaut*

conquering of the serpent/dragon by a god or saint – representatives of the new world order. Depending on context, the dragon is vanquished e.g. by Apollo, Kadmos, Perseus, Siegfried, Saint George, or Archangel Michael.

The defeat of the dragon does not only signify the triumph over chaos and the foundation of the new world order, but also the repression of the primeval instincts – recognized as dark, evil and unwanted. These forces usually have a destructive character but when we learn to master them, they become a tool of transformation, spiritual enlightenment and liberation. The traditional mythological story of a victorious fight with the dragon/serpent is not a tale about taming the force but about rejecting and denying it. Rejected instincts emerge from the forgotten abyss of the inner mind, bringing chaos into the life of man and assuming shapes of dragon-like and serpent-like monsters. The mastery of this force, however, is possible through spiritual discipline: we can learn to rule over the forgotten aspects of the mind and use them in our spiritual progress.

A Few Thoughts on Tiamat

Adam

> "Naught but Tiamat remained.
> The Great Serpent, the Enormous Worm
> The Snake with iron teeth
> The Snake with sharpened claw
> The Snake with Eyes of Death."
> *(Magan Text, Necronomicon)*

I. Enuma Elish and the Origins of Tiamat

The central work of the Babylonian mythology, which presents the origin of the universe and creation of humans, is *Enuma Elish*, the epic that was titled after the first two written words, meaning: "When in the height." The oldest version of this text, written on seven tablets, is dated as originating from the first half of the first millennium BCE, i.e. the period which, according to modern historians, was the final stage of forming Babylonian and Assyrian views on the cosmological creation of the world. In the first millennium BCE the final image of the physical world appeared. The earth was believed to have the shape of a flat disk, with stars and the sky above it, and with the cosmic waters and the underworld below. The underworld, as the place inhabited by the dead, was envisioned as a waterless desert, full of dust and darkness, which suggests that it was located below the ocean of the cosmic waters.

The *Enuma Elish* myth leaves us with a complete picture of the creation of the world and establishment of the world order in gradual stages: from chaos to the most organized creation: the man. Other cosmogonic texts present only a few chosen aspects of this issue. The world begins with gods who embody particular cosmic elements and ever-existing forces of nature that come into being by the creative force of Marduk. The work is then an expression of the official doctrine of Babylonian priests. For this reason, it is worthwhile to think whether the creation of the world, even though depicted so elaborately, is the actual goal of the text itself. The emotional value is attached to the parts which describe the birth and maturation of Marduk, and also his preparations for the fight with Tiamat. This is followed by the parts about the war itself and finally, the glorification of the triumphant god. Thus, we may assume that the epic is in fact a literary hymn to worship Marduk, the major deity of the Babylonian pantheon, the creator of heaven and earth, the lord of the world.

We encounter Tiamat for the first time when, similarly as the ancient Babylonians, we ask what was in the beginning, when the gods did not yet exist. Once, as the legend has it, there were only ancient, primordial beings. In the beginning there was nothing apart from Apsu, the primeval ocean of fresh waters (Hebrew: Tehom, which is seen by some researchers as a derivative of the name Tiamat – the depth). At this stage we also encounter Mummu – the concept that may be interpreted as a thought-creative life force, or as one of the names or titles of Tiamat. The goddess herself is presented in the myth in diverse aspects. Evidently, she symbolizes the primordial chaos and the dynamic force of creation. On the one hand, she is a caring and understanding mother of the creatures whom she gave birth to (she passionately opposes Apsu's idea to punish the young careless gods). On the other hand, she is presented as a warrior goddess of blood and vengeance, and the mother of all evil and monsters. Also her shape is not actually defined in the epic. Generally, she is depicted as an enormous creature, capable of taking seven winds into her body, and out of which Marduk will finally create the whole physical world. From other sources, however, we find that the goddess was most often portrayed as a great dragon or serpent, representing the salty waters of the ocean.

Before we discuss the detailed descriptions of the particular aspects and qualities of Tiamat, we can for a moment reflect on what might have been the basis of such a presentation of this myth. First of all, the attention should be turned to the historical processes and the cultural context. The myth may originate from the old Babylonian period, in the circle of the priests of Marduk, and its original function was to legitimize the importance of the patriarchal god of Babylon, the kingdom of a minor significance at that time. This occurred due to the political changes in Mesopotamia that were happening at this period of time. On the other hand, the myth might refer to the conflict between the matriarchal and patriarchal rules of the social and religious structures, just as it was in Egypt, where the cult of the lunar female goddess Taurt (Taweret) (her Greek counterpart is Typhon) was degraded by the dominant solar cult, and then demonized and associated with all that was dark and evil. According to another interpretation, this symbolic transformation of chaos (the unstructured principle) into cosmos (the organized structure) might represent the rise of culture and its opposition against nature. Man has always been striving to tame and control what he could not understand and what threatened him, paradoxically, still being bound to it, like to a mother.

II. Goddess of Primordial Chaos and All Creation

"When in the height heaven was not named,
And the earth beneath did not yet bear a name,
And the primeval Apsu, who begat them,
And Mummu-Tiamat, the mother of them both."
(Enuma Elish)

First and foremost, Tiamat is the primordial and chaotic source of all life. It is from her womb that the first couple of gods (Lahmu and Lahamu) emerge, and they in turn give birth to all other gods. Moreover, in the eighth verse of *Enuma Elish* we read that this happened when none of the gods "bore a name, and no destinies were ordained," which suggests that Tiamat is not merely a shapeless source of all life but also possesses the power to shape and create destinies. This is reflected in the further part of the myth, when she creates her demonic armies and gives Kingu the Tablets of Destiny. In this aspect she resembles the Greek Gaia, who – according to Hesiod – was not created by any god but came into being herself, emerging from Chaos. We may assume that in this conception chaos contains within itself also the inner cosmic essence that aims at some form of order. Also, similarly to Gaia, she is the caring mother for her children and strongly opposes the idea of punishment for their unworthy deeds. Another quality of "mother Hubur who bore all beings" is her typically watery character. Without water there is no life, and this gave water a special role in all possible mythologies. On the one hand, just like in the Egyptian myths in which Nun is the primeval ocean and symbol of the watery chaos, Tiamat represents the watery womb in which all gods and all life come into being. On the other hand, Tiamat is the great monster, the Dragon, the one who rules the source of this life-giving elixir.

However, Tiamat is not only the source of all creative energy and the mother of gods, but also of the whole world in general. Transition from shapeless watery element to a stable land appears in myths as an important act, essential to transformation of chaos into cosmos. The next step in this process is separation of heaven from earth, which perhaps is the same as the first act of creation, if we take into consideration the initial identification of the heaven with the oceans of the world. In *Enuma Elish* we read: "Then the lord rested, gazing upon her dead body, he divided the flesh and devised a cunning plan. He split her up like a flat fish into two halves; One half of her he established as a covering for heaven. He fixed a bolt, he stationed a watchman, and bade them not to let her waters come forth." And thus heaven and earth were created. Such an image of the primeval water from which earth emerges or is created is universal and can be found in almost all world mythologies. More rarely do we encounter (as typical examples we may point at the Scandinavian or Persian mythology) a motif of the rise of the world from polarization of two elements – water or earth and fire. The cosmogonic function of fire is generally ambiguous as it exists on the border between culture and nature, but this is not the theme of this essay.

As the mother of all, Tiamat can also be viewed from another perspective. If we follow Erich Fromm's suggestion, perhaps we could look at the *Enuma Elish* myth through the mirror of modern psychology. Like in the concept of a conflict between the social structure and religious cults, also this time the significance of the male and the female principle might be the key to understanding the symbolism of the epic. The cult of the great goddess has always been connected with the symbolism of nature and fertility. This belief was associated with the mystical qualities of a woman. Maternity and the ability to give new life belonged to the sphere of sacrum. In the history of religion, the period of the cult of mother goddess is called the lunar phase. Female energy embodied the most primeval forces of nature, the power of creation and fertility. Also Marduk, in order to defeat Tiamat, proved that he possessed the power of creation. Hence, the scene of the ordeal in the myth (the symbolism of which is thoroughly analyzed by Fromm) in which Marduk, at the feast in the palace, has to cause a robe to disappear and then appear again. He must do this with the power of his word. In later, more modern cosmological myths (like e.g. the Bible) we encounter male, solar gods who create the world exactly in this way – by means of their word. Curiously, even the process of giving birth will be changed. Instead of being born from a woman, it will be the man that will give birth to her: like in the case of Adam and Eve, or Zeus and Athena.

III. Darkness, Blood and Vengeance

"Mummu-Hubur, who formed all things,
Hath made in addition weapons invincible;
she hath spawned monster-serpents,
Sharp of tooth and merciless of fang.
With poison, instead of blood, she hath filled their bodies
With splendor she hath decked them; she hath made them
of lofty stature..."
(*Enuma Elish*)

In the further part of the epic we see Tiamat from a completely different perspective. This time she is the one who takes life away, avenges Apsu, and becomes the mother of all evil and all monsters. She creates and takes a new lover, gives him the mastery of destiny (the Tablets of Destiny) and fills him with her own blood, from which man will be created later. She is now liberated, strong and independent. Let us now address what influenced this radical change.

As we have already mentioned, attention should be given to anxiety occurring within the new conceptions of a religious cult, social structures, or psychology. However, as Mircea Eliade points out, the whole character of *Enuma Elish* is quite gloomy and dark. Tiamat is not only the chaotic whole that preceded all creation, but eventually she appears as the creator of all monsters. Her "creativity" is now completely negative. This is confirmed by the verse: "Evil she wrought against the gods, her children. To avenge Apsu, Tiamat planned evil." We might thus assume that she was the creator of evil and it had not existed before. The primordiality is then presented as a source of all negative emanations.

On the other hand, we may trace the process of evolution from chaos to cosmos, as it is suggested by Eleazar Mieletinski. From this point of view, the transformation of chaos into cosmos, i.e. darkness into light, or disorder into order, usually occurs in the form of a fight between an archaic hero with chthonic demons and monsters. A popular motif is the cosmic fight with the serpent (dragon), the goal of which is the defeat of primordial chaos. The serpent (dragon) in many mythologies is connected with waters and often presented as a threat to humans – bringer of flood or drought, or generally – the one who introduces the element of chaos and disrupts the balance of the world.

Anyway, mythological conflicts and duels almost all have some sort of cosmological nature and symbolize the defeat of chaos by the forces of cosmos. It is not, however, characteristic only of the Babylonian mythology. In the Scandinavian lore, the gods Thor, Odin and others fight chthonic monsters: Jormungandr, the wolf Fenrir, or the goddess of death, Hel. In the Egyptian mythology, Atum-

Re everyday faces the underworld serpent Apep. In Greece we encounter the struggle between Zeus and Typhon, the father of such chthonic monsters as Hydra of Lerne, Chimera, Cerberus, or the two-headed dog Orpho. Even in the Bible we can find notes about the conflict between God and the dragon or a fish, also representing the eternal element of chaos (Rahab, Tehom, Leviathan). Many other similar couples can be mentioned - like Apollo and Python, Tretona and Azi-Dahaka, or Kersasp and Sruwar.

Another important motif in *Enuma Elish* is the concept of Tiamat's blood. Even though neglected by many researchers, this motif is essential to the full understanding of the nature of the goddess. Its significance is suggested in two quotations: "Let the wind carry her blood into secret places" and "He cut through the channels of her blood, and he made the North wind bear it away into secret places." From these words we may assume that all Tiamat's essence and the creative element of chaos is contained within her blood. The god of light must therefore hide it to finish the process of transformation from chaos to cosmos. Moreover, also humans are created from Tiamat's blood, as she is the mother and the lover of Kingu, whose blood is the substance from which Marduk creates humanity. As Eliade notices, man is therefore created from demonic matter. Kingu, even though being one of the first gods, was also the archdemon and the commander of the army of all monsters created by Tiamat. Besides, the very role of man in the Sumerian and Babylonian mythology is pitiful: mankind is created and exists only to serve the gods. The name "Lullu" attributed to man may be translated as "a savage" or "a weak one." According to Mieletinski, the prototypical creation of the world from a slain creature occurs through sacrifice. Probably, in the more archaic mythologies, we would find more tales about creation of the animals and plants, heavenly bodies and other natural objects, from the flesh of a slain "ancestor." The motif of blood sacrifice is evident in the Aztec mythology – the gods need human blood to stay alive. This is also reflected in the Babylonian epic - the gods need Kingu's blood to purify themselves after the war is finished and to create mankind. Even the good will of Marduk, who holds power over life and is called "lord of sacred hymns, resurrecting the dead," is not enough. To create life one needs blood, the seat of the creative element of chaos and all life.

IV. Tiamat in the Necronomicon

"Know that Tiamat seeks ever to rise to the stars,
and when the Upper is united to the Lower,
then a new Age will come of Earth,
and the Serpent shall be made whole,
and the Waters will be as One,
when on high the heavens had not been named."
(*Necronomicon*)

In the lecture given in 1982 at the Magick Childe Shop, Simon described the origin of his Necronomicon as an ancient Sumerian religion. Even though this is a highly controversial claim, it might help to define the role and the qualities of Tiamat in the so called "Cthulhu Mythos." Curiously, the core of Simon's work is the "Magan Text," a reflection of the *Enuma Elish* epic, although from a little bit different perspective.

If we look closer at the picture of Tiamat we can evidently see that a greater emphasis is put on her role as the Queen of the Ancient Ones than as the mother of the Elder Gods. She has characteristic chthonic qualities as the mother of all evil and plagues that arise from the underworld. She becomes the one who functions not merely as a primordial chaos, the source of all, but also as the goddess who demands blood to be spilt in her name – in order to awaken her from the sleep in the caverns of the earth. It seems logical, as Simon argues that she might be identified with the Sumerian goddess of the underworld, Ereshkigal, whose name means "Lady of the Great Below." As for the meaning of the name Magan, he proposes a theory that it might be translated as "The Place of Death" (which suggests a place of transformation rather than the absolute end).

Generally, the author of this version of the Necronomicon goes further to say that Tiamat may be also identified with serpent figures such as Leviathan, or Tehom, while the other chaotic principle Apsu - with Cthulhu. It is significant as it points at her universal dragon-like character, closely connected with water, but also with all other elements. What proves this theory is a great number of references to the ancient cult of the serpent (and thus, Tiamat) in Simon's Necronomicon. It is also reflected in the quotation that opens this subchapter, which presents a suggestive picture of the dragon symbol as a being that transcends all concepts and oppositions, and at the same time is the greatest force of all, as it contains everything within.

We can also discuss the association of this theory with the number 11 that often appears both in *Enuma Elish* and the "Magan Text" as a reference to some of the goddess' aspects (in the first case, it is the number of monsters created by Tiamat to fight the gods of light and order, which may point at how the adept of the Left Hand Path can transcend one step further; in the second case, it is the number of the blood sacrifices which should be made to awaken the goddess from her sleep). In the simplest interpretation, the number 11 signifies the final and forbidden unity as it is formed from the microcosm (the number 5) with the macrocosm (the number 6).

The last element that should be discussed to understand Tiamat's association with the Necronomicon and the Ancient Ones, is the motif of blood. This time it becomes even more important than in *Enuma Elish*. It is no longer a mere essence from which man is created, or a substance containing the chaotic creative element of the universe. Now it is described as the gate to the world of darkness and the human potential to become as gods themselves.

If we decide to accept *Enuma Elish* and the "Magan Text" as two complementary parts of one whole, we encounter the following image:

In the "Magan Text" we read:

"He split the sundered Tiamat in twain
And fashioned the heavens and the earth,
With a Gate to keep the Ancient Ones Without.
With a Gate whose Key is hid forever."

In *Enuma Elish*:

"Let the wind carry her blood into secret places."
"He cut through the channels of her blood, and he made the North wind bear it away into secret places."

If we connect it with the story of the creation of man, we do not have to think long where the key is hidden. Later on, this question is answered also in the further part of the "Magan Text:" "Man is the key by which the Gate of Iak Sakkak may be flung wide." Therefore, blood is this element that links humans with the Ancient Ones and is the reason why the world of Creation is inseparably connected with Darkness and Chaos, as it contains the primordial principle that is the force contained within human blood.

V. Conclusion

The nature of the goddess Tiamat is probably one of the most complicated cases in all mythologies. We can find analagous examples in ancient archetypal force of the mother goddess like Gaia, as well as in the chthonic forces, like Ereshkigal. On the one hand, she personifies the creative energy in nature, on the other – its final doom and darkness.

Looking at this issue from another perspective, we see a completely different picture. We see Tiamat as an archetypal symbol of the Dragon: the force that transcends all dualities and leads man toward the final forbidden unity.

But even then we may take a step further: Tiamat is also the force belonging to this world. If we, however, follow the Necronomicon theories, we might assume that her essence exists beyond the angles and dimensions known to man, between the Tree of Life and the Tree of Night. Her blood is the key which opens all gates – and the eternal promise that was given to mankind. This cannot be surprising, though, if we remember that the evolution on the true path has neither a beginning nor an end.

Bibliography:

1. Krystyna Łyczkowska i Krystyna Szarzyńska: *Mitologia Mezopotamii*
2. Mircea Eliade: *The Creation of World in Enuma Elish*
3. Eleazar Mieletinski: *Chaos i kosmos. Kosmogeneza*
4. Erich Fromm: *Mit o stworzeniu świata*
5. Jean-Paul Roux: *Creative Blood in Mesopotamia*
6. H.W.F. Saggs: *Enuma Elish*

7. *Enuma Elish*
8. Simon: *Necronomicon*

Apep - The Serpent Chaos Demon

Asenath Mason

The name "Apophis" translates as "the great serpent," and indeed, he was the Egyptian demon in the form of a serpent. He dwelled in the underground dark realm of Amenti. According to legends, he was born from saliva of the ancient Egyptian goddess Neith in the waters of Nun – the primeval ocean, embodiment of primordial waters, out of which everything emerged. He was most often presented as a huge water snake – standing near a deity who pierced him with a knife or other weapons. This image depicted the defeat of the serpent and the act of establishing control over his demonic powers by benevolent gods. Therefore, his role is similar to one of other mythological serpents and sea dragons encountered in the whole world. For instance, the Mesopotamian dragon goddess Tiamat, or the Biblical serpent Leviathan. In a similar way, Apep personified the primordial Chaos, darkness existing outside of the order of ma'at. He belonged to the sphere outside the world created and structured by gods.

It was believed that Apep is 16 meters long, his body is black, and his skin is rough. His roaring shakes the whole underworld. His name can also be translated as "He who was Spat Out," which refers to the legend about his birth.

He was also called "Evil Lizard," "Opponent of Ra," "World Encircler," and also "Serpent of Rebirth."

Apep is the "adversary" disrupting the divine cosmic order. Every day he attempts to stop the solar barque of the Sun God Ra and imprison him forever in the darkness of the underworld. His power is so great that nothing can defeat him. And even when he is defeated, this is only for a short period of time, because the following day he rises again in order to threaten the solar barque during its voyage through Amenti. He awaits it on the mountain of Bakhu, and when the sun god approaches the mountain, every day during the seventh hour of the night, Apep tries to devour the barque. He also attempts to stop the barque by drinking the whole water from the underground river, and to hinder its passage by means of his coils, called "sandbanks."

Therefore, Ra does not set on his journey alone but with other gods, who help him protect the barque. Among them we can find Shu, the solar god who holds up the firmament and separates it from the earth. Legend has it that he was the second divine pharaoh after Ra. The followers of Apep plotted against him and attacked him in his palace at At Nub. Shu managed to defeat them, but then his own followers revolted against him. Then Shu abdicated and left his throne to his son Geb, after which he returned to the skies. But he was not the only god who protected the barque. Among the defenders we can find Maahes, the lion-god of war, representing all forces of the fiery sky, also called the "lord of slaughter." On the solar barque there was also the goddess Selket who protected it by means of her magic spells. There was also Mehen, a serpentine deity, and the goddesses Isis and Neith. All of them helped to protect the barque from Apep's threats and used their powers to defeat him. Because of their efforts, Apep is caught in a magical net and then cut with knives or pierced with a spear by Horus (in some versions of the myth his body is sliced and then burnt). His blood paints the sky red and announces the rise of the barque from the darkness of the night at sunrise.

The only god who is strong enough to slay Apep is Set, another deity with ambiguous features. When Apep swallows the solar barque, Set and Mehen kill the Serpent and cut his body so that the barque can come out of it. Texts that describe the "defeat of Apep" also mention the conversation that occurs between him and Set who captured him into the net. The Serpent tries to convince Set to let him go and reminds him that the sun gods are also his enemies because they fought against him (Apep reminds him that Set lost his genitals in the fight with Horus). Furious at these words, Set kills Apep. As a symbol of the forces of darkness, however, Set is often identified with the Serpent of Chaos. Some texts even mention their names alternately as a symbolic enemy of the sun and as the lord of darkness. The defeat of Set or Apep is thus a symbolic triumph over darkness and its aspects which assume the form of dark gods, shadows, and other demons of the underworld.

In a few paintings Apep is presented as defeated by the god Ra himself - in the form of the Great Cat of Iunu he cuts off the Serpent's head under the sacred tree of Ished or under the sycamore tree. Also magical spells used in protection against Apep referred to his defeat by the solar gods. The incantations mentioned him being sliced, burnt, and destroyed, and also his wax statue was cut into pieces and burnt. This happened due to the belief that Apep threatens not only gods but also humans. He was responsible for solar eclipses, when the night fell during the day, and also for storms and earthquakes. To help in the fight with Apep, in the temple of Amen-Ra in Waset the priests performed a special ritual during which the Serpent was symbolically slain, sliced and burnt in the end.

Kenneth Grant in *Nightside of Eden* suggests that the name "Apep" can be traced to an African concept of Afefe, "the wind." According to this theory, the name refers to the most primeval picture of a serpent as an emblem of the creative spiritual force:

"The Afefe-Apophis is also the origin of the Fafnir Worm of Norse myth, and, as Massey has shown, a modern derivative is our word 'puff,' to blow out' in the sense of becoming big, swollen, tumescent or pregnant. The African Afefe therefore reveals the 'bellying' or billowing force of the wind that is the gust or ghost which became - in a later recension of the Mysteries - the Holy Ghost that impregnates the virgin in the form of the Dove, the typical bird of the air. This is further corroborated by the fact that the genius of the wind, of which Afefe is the 'messenger,' dwells in the grand temple of Legba, the African phallic deity that in the later cults was equated with evil owing to his connection with the mysteries of sex."

In the symbolic sense, Apep is thus the force of destruction, darkness and non-being. He can be identified with the Void, "the black hole" swallowing everything, existing completely outside the world of nature – in what Kenneth Grant calls Universe B. He is the Black Dragon, the force of death, the primordial energy that existed before the concept of time and space appeared. His existence is characterized by cyclic process: the attack, the fight with the sun gods, death, rebirth, and again the attack. He cannot be destroyed or fully defeated – he is the eternal and infinite aspect of Chaos.

Ceremony of Apep

Various Authors

Envision the sun disappearing behind the horizon, into the jaws of the Serpent-Dragon of the Underworld. While focusing on this vision, start vibrating the mantra: "Lepaca Apep." When you feel the atmosphere around you is changing and becoming tense, face the direction of west and begin the ceremony:

I, (magical name), invoke Apep, demonic Serpent of the Underworld!
Devourer of the sun on its journey through the sea of night and adversary of the gods of light!
Ruler of the seventh hour of the soul's descent into Amenti!
You transform the sunlight into the void of the Black Sun.
Your blood paints the sky red.
I invoke you! Come forth at my calling!
I seek to unite with your force,
To rest in your coils,
To enter the land of the dead that is your kingdom.
Come to me, demon of waters and fire!
Lord of life behind the veil of death!
Rise out of the infernal abyss and embrace me with your coils!

Apep! Apepi! Aapep! Apofis! Set! Tyfon!

I summon you in the name of Darkness and Light, Fire and Water, which are your essence! Hear my calling and rise from the abyss of the Underworld, from the underground land of Amenti!

Lepaca Apep!
Lepaca Apofis!
Lepaca Drakon!

May this calling shake the deepest pits of hell!

Ho Drakon Ho Megas!

Envision that you are on a voyage on the solar barque through an underground river. It gets darker and darker around you. Suddenly Apep appears in front of you. He drinks all the water up and swallows the barque. You are now inside his body. Feel how you become one with the Serpent. Inflame yourself in the power of magic that rises in you. You are the unity of shadow and light, life and death. You shine with the light that illuminates the Void and the darkness of the abyss. Gradually you are filled up with divinity. Meditate upon this feeling.

When you feel that it is time to end the meditation, close the ceremony.

In the Desert of Sutuach
Killed, Dismembered and Resurrected from Flames

Holger Kliemannel

"Who calleth me evil, knoweth not the extent of my darkness."
Nebet-Het, mistress of the temple

Prerogative

In the whole Egyptian pantheon there is no character as versatile and also as misunderstood as Sutuach, better known today under the name Seth. Once a god of the sea who became the god of the empire, he gradually turned into a desert god, who was sometimes worshipped in non-permanent oasis areas. Some kings, for instance Sethos I and Sethos II as well as Sethnacht, held the name Seth as a proper name, thus subordinating to his physical and magical powers.

Up to the 4th dynasty he was the great god of initiation, transformation and expansion. Into this time falls the building of the pyramids of Giseh and Sakkara. The Egyptian name for the pyramid[14] was besides "mer"

---

[14] The word "pyramid" derives from the Greek „pyramis," meaning „wheatcake."

- 89 -

(instrument of ascension) also "Seth-mount." To understand the heart of the dark god, one looked up into the sun in the South. Seth was particularly popular in the 19th and 20th dynasties, during the time when Egypt extended its empire and when prosperity flowed through the country. When the empire slowly fell apart in the 22nd dynasty and could not withstand the pressure from outside any longer, Seth's prestige was diminished.

It was only with the growing influence of the Greeks in the Egyptian empire that Sethianism was revived. The Greeks brought a new idea with them, which was alien to the Egyptians, the idea of the individual and of personal freedom. Until then, everything in the everyday life of the Egyptian people was centered on the pharaoh. The alien idea of the free individual was assigned to the desert god of the foreign parts,[15] Seth, who played a role again from then on, and he was brought to Greece in the form of Egyptian magic by Greek philosophers who studied in Egypt. In the course of time the Greeks associated Seth with the Titan Typhon in the form of Typhon-Seth-Heh, who is a precursor of the Christian-Judaic Satan. In ancient Egypt, the 6th hour of the day was assigned to Seth, and this hour plays an important role in today's Sethianism as well.

Thus, Seth has not only become an important god in mythology again, but due to his identification with freedom of the individual he turned into the adversary. The newly won freedom through Seth was used to find and recognize oneself. The monotheistic religions totally submit themselves to their god and make themselves his slaves.

---

[15] Foreigners, i.e. Non-Egyptians, had to wander through the desert in order to reach the centres of Egypt. Therefore, Egyptians associated the desert with the foreign parts, and thus Seth as a desert god was the god of the foreign parts.

The word of God is not questioned. Not so with Seth. He is a god of those who are becoming. He opposes submission. His nature comprises clearly Luciferian aspects. Seth, like Satan, is the prosecutor, the stumbling block of the status quo that breaks the tendency to stagnation. According to C.G. Jung, even the Jews refused to worship the light god of the Egyptians, Osiris, during their Egyptian captivity. Instead, they worshipped a donkey's head depicting the adversary of Osiris, Seth. In order to eradicate these old, in Moses' eyes pagan, habits from his tribe, it was necessary to wander through the desert for 40 years, because only this way he could ensure that only his monotheistic belief would be practiced in his new land, for the old people and their religion would have died in the meantime.

Seth brings chaos into the hearts that helps us escape from our everyday life in order to "become." Seth is the companion in the foreign parts, in the wastelands, in the darkness, a friend on the way. At the same time he is the initiator, the great questioner of the achievements, the spanner in the works or, as the Germans say, the sand in the gear. When you are standing at the edge of the world, he will you push you onward.

This is only a short summary of Seth's characteristics. As he is sufficiently well-known I will spare myself the detailed portrayal of Seth and the interpretation of his nature.

Attuning

Stand upright and make the sign of Seth-Typhon while reading the following words:

Seth teaches you not to sacrifice.
Seth teaches you to hark to the prophecies.

Seth teaches you to determine your own fate.
Seth teaches you to live freely.
Seth teaches you to fight proudly.
Seth teaches you to be like a flying arrow: unwavering.
Seth teaches you to reject.
Seth teaches you to dedicate yourself.
Seth teaches you to stand by your heart.
Seth teaches you to make your arms become cobras ready for a fight.
Seth teaches you to defend your work.
Seth teaches you to make your gaze strong like HIS eye amidst the desert storm.
Seth teaches you to eat your gods as Unas once did.
Seth teaches you to drink their blood and to dance on their bones.
Seth teaches you to shatter their golden statues.
Seth teaches you to offer their bloody hearts to the stars.
Their hearts shall strengthen your heart, their brains shall inspire your thoughts, their blood shall turn your blood to boiling lava.
Seth teaches you not to return to the place of your origin.
Seth teaches you to go out by the day.
Seth teaches you to become ice.
Seth teaches you to become a stone.
Seth teaches you to become a flame.
Seth teaches you to become a calm sea and on-storming flood.
Seth teaches you to be a refuge of your conviction.
Seth teaches you to be a battleship amidst the tides of fate.
Seth teaches you that no freedom is given to you.
Seth teaches you that he is not your master.
Seth teaches you that your chains are your teachers.
Seth teaches you that every experience carries you beyond the union with the Red One.
Seth teaches you that every experience makes you a god, radiant and indestructible, the center and sputtering well of life itself.
Eat your gods, son of the black star!

Invocation

Sit in the dragon-asana. Speak the following invocation:

Lepaca Seth!

Seth is the Son of the Way.
Seth is the Lord of Death.
Seth is the Tree of the Senses.
Seth is the Seed of Hell.
Seth is the Word of the Night.
Seth is the Blood of Consecration.

O Seth, whirl the wheel and shake the world, god of all
gods, who shall abide until the end of time.
The gates are wide open for thee at this secret place.
Rise, eternal Seth, shake off the dust of time that separates
us.
To us, the wanderers on the Draconian Path,
come forth and show thyself in thy true form.

Seth is the Seed of the Way.
Seth is the Son of Death.
Seth is the Lord of the Senses.
Seth is the Tree of Hell.
Seth is the Blood of the Night.
Seth is the Word of Consecration.

Thy secret name is "He Who Chooses."
Choose me, who in strength shall rise.
I am a god, a becoming one.
I call thee, o Seth, into the wide landscapes of my temple.
I shall come into existence by my own power.
I am a pilgrim in times of fire.
I am a pilgrim in times of water.
I am a pilgrim in times of air.
I am a pilgrim in times of earth.

I am the one who walketh the desert.
I am the one who swimmeth across the seas.
I am the one who riseth into the air on the wings of the
Horus-Hawk.
I am the one whose claws churn up the earth.

Seth is the Son of the Way.
Seth is the Germ of Death.
Seth is the Seed of the Senses.
Seth is the Lord of Hell.
Seth is the Son of the Night.
Seth is the Tree of Consecration.

I am the living embodiment of thy will by doing my true
will.
I recognize thee with thy own eyes, Typhon-Seth.
I command my own becoming.
This is my will, the only and true will of (magical name)!

HO DRAKON HO MEGAS!

Meditation

Close your eyes and sit down on the ground in the dragon-asana. Feel the ground. It becomes warm, warmer and warmer, until it is all hot. You open your eyes, the sun blinds you; you need a few moments before you can perceive your surroundings. You realize that you are in the desert, sitting on the hot sand. Above you, vultures are circling, there is nobody to see. No animal, not a plant, only hot, dry desert sand. The air is flickering with heat. Your throat is aching with thirst, your blood is boiling, and the heat becomes an endless torment for your body. You look down on yourself and see that you are nude. The body is marked by the heat. It is glaring red, dried out and strewn with blisters. You gather your last strength, rise and intonate quietly LEPACA SETH, over and over again, until you see a vortex forming in your Ajna-chakra. It opens, but not as an eye, but rather as a deep, black hole. As soon as it has opened fully, Seth jumps out and looks at you with fiery, bloodthirsty eyes. In his left hand you recognize a chalice, in his right hand he holds a silvery sharp sword, glinting in the sun. He takes the sword and raises it for the deadly strike. Exactly in that moment your consciousness jumps over, into him. Now you see your body standing in front of you, the form of your life. You see how small it is.

You strike and see your head separating from the body and falling into the hot desert sand. The body sinks to the ground, blood spurts from the lifeless body and sinks into the sand immediately.

The vultures pounce on your dead body, peck out the eyes, hack around in the open mouth, greedily rip the red flesh from the body with their beaks, and devour all flesh. Little by little they devour your heart, your lungs, liver, tear open the stomach and devour all your organs until nothing is left but your bare bones.

You turn away from your skeleton and put the blood-smeared sword in the sand. You seize the chalice with both hands and look deep into it. The chalice contains a viscid, night-black liquid, in which nothing is reflected. Your consciousness slides into the chalice, and now you see Seth above you, staring at you with a firm gaze. He opens his mouth and a flame shoots forth and penetrates you. You are the fire that spreads at the speed of lightning. You do not feel anything any longer except the fire. You are one with the flames inside you, and you are the fire that surrounds you.

The fire goes out, and amidst the last flaring flames you are standing in your true form, whatever it may look like. Seth is standing opposite you, looking at you. In his right hand he holds the Uas-scepter, in his left hand the Ankh-cross.

After a while he presents to you the scepter of rule and of magic power that you take with the right hand and hold it up. Then Seth presents to you the Ankh-cross of eternity, which you hold downward after taking it. While you are standing like this, with the scepter held up high and Ankh-cross held downward, he puts a ribbon of cloth around your forehead, on which a serpent is depicted. He pulls the headband very tight and you feel a pressure in your head.

Suddenly the serpent begins to move and becomes alive. It bites into its own tail, thus enclosing your head, and in doing so it grows very quickly, and your mind begins to grow with it. Your mind becomes bigger, wider, infinitely wide, bigger than you have ever been, wider than the desert of Seth; wider than the land. This should be a flash-like impulse, at whose end you open your eyes equally quick and find yourself in your temple in the dragon-asana.

Allow, whatever may come.

Closing

Finish the working with the words:

Seth is the Son of the Way.
Seth is the Lord of Death.
Seth is the Tree of the Senses.
Seth is the Seed of Hell.
Seth is the Word of the Night.
Seth is the Blood of Consecration.
I am Seth.
I have looked into his blazing eyes and seen myself.

In my heart is Khephra.
In my heart is Maat.
In my heart is Geb.
In my heart is Nuit.

The wanderer of a high degree is constantly going the way.
The wanderer of a medium degree is going the way from
time to time.
The wanderer of a low degree is not going the way.
But who is without degree denies the way and derides the
wanderers loudly.
Nothing is worthy to be made a way
if none is found to deride it.

To the wanderer of a low degree the way is an obstacle.
To the wanderer of a medium degree the way is a pastime.
To the wanderer of a high degree the way is a challenge.
The wanderer of the highest degree IS the way.
Seth is my way.

The Kingdom of Seker

Asenath Mason

Seker (also spelt Sokar, Sokaris, and Socharis) was an ancient god worshipped in Memphis. He was the patron god of the necropolis and was known as "the one who is on the sand." The necropolis of Sakkara was named after him. The cult of Seker was one of the oldest in Egypt and in its earliest forms it represented certain aspects of the afterlife. It was believed that he represented the act of separation of the *Ba* from the *Ka* – the soul from the physical body, which occurred after death. The statues of Seker were therefore placed in tombs, together with *The Book of the Dead*, in order to ensure that the separation of the soul would be successful. The oldest account of Seker worship dates to the 18th or 19th Dynasty but there might have been older. As we read in the commentary to *The Book of Amduat*, the priests of Thebes removed all texts, figures or details which they found inconvenient for their views. In Thebes, Seker had a festival dedicated to him. It was known as the Henu Festival, in which his statue was carried in a barque, representing the ferry that carried the dead through particular parts of the underworld.

The religion of Seker described this god as a principle of impenetrable darkness, of the region of sand, guarded by terrible monster serpents, the land where all tortures and suffering awaited the dead sinners. It was the realm of fire, roughly corresponding to the vision of hell developed later by Christianity. It was later, probably in the Middle Kingdom, that Seker became associated with Ptah, the god of craftsmen and reincarnation. Seker's identity was subsumed into that of Ptah, becoming Ptah-Seker, and eventually it came to embrace another god of death, Osiris, and became Ptah-Seker-Osiris.

In *The Book of Amduat* we find an extensive description of the kingdom of Seker. The text itself is also called *The Book of the Secret Chamber* and describes the journey of the Sun God through the underworld. Just as the Sun "dies" in the west and has to pass through the dangerous Realm of the Night, so the soul has to pass through the Secret Chamber, the land of death, and defeat its enemies with the help of spiritual guardians in order to become reborn as a living god. The journey is divided into 12 "hours," corresponding to the divisions of the underworld and the twelve hours of the night. The passage through the realm of Seker includes two divisions of the Duat: the fourth and the fifth. There, the solar barque of the traveler has to pass through dangerous, dark and rough way through the realm of utmost darkness. The land is formed of barren, sandy deserts, inhabited by monster serpents with two or three heads, and some of them with wings. All other boats from the procession have to turn back and the barque is left alone. There is no water and the barque has to be towed by souls of the dead inhabitants of other regions. The boat transforms itself into a huge serpent with a fiery breath which shines in the dark and threatens enemies away, and only in this shape does it manage to pass through this dark kingdom.

The main corridor in this land is called Re-Stau, and it is a desert environment. At the end of the first section of it there is the door Mates-Sma-Ta, the second section - the door Mates-Mau-At, and the third section - the door Mates-En-Neheh. There is also an inscription from which we find that it is the road by which the body of Seker enters, and that his form is neither seen nor perceived. The name of this (fourth) division is Ankhet-Kheperu, and that of its Gate is Ament-Sethau, while the goddess of the hour is called Urt-Em-Sekhemu-S (In *The Book of Amduat* each level, each part of it, and each gate has its own name, as well as the equivalent god, guardian, and all creatures which dwell there). The fifth hour of the Duat, the kingdom of Seker itself, also has its own names and attributes. The hour is called Ament and contains secret ways and doors of the hidden chamber of Seker. The main gate is called Aha-Neteru, the gods are called Baiu-Ammiu-Tuat, and the goddess of the hour is Semit-Her-Abt-Uaa-S.

Seker is depicted as a hawk-headed man, who stands between a pair of wings that project from the back of a huge serpent with two heads and necks, and a tail terminating in a bearded human head. This description can be found in *The Book of Amduat*. Later, Seker became depicted as a mummified human who was falcon-headed and had green skin, representing the concept of rebirth.

The following meditation was constructed on the basis of the description from *The Book of Amduat*. It corresponds to the fifth hour, where the soul passes through the realm of Seker, together with his secret chamber. It might be memorized and performed as a solitary working, or it might be led by another person.

Into the Realm of Death
Meditation

Asenath Mason

Sit in a comfortable position and begin visualization.

Envision yourself standing in front of a huge gate. The gate is protected by two strong walls, with a passage running between them. This passage is swept by flames of fire. The gate is guarded by nine gods. At the entrance to the corridor and at its exit stands a jackal-headed god. The name of the serpent-guard is Teka-Hra. Greet him by saying his name and the words: "Ho Drakon Ho Megas," and ask him to let you pass. The passage will open for you and you will be allowed to enter.

You are now in the desert land. Around you there is only darkness and you cannot see anything apart from the glowing eyes of demons which lurk there. On one side you can see a serpent named Tepan, who presents to the god his daily offerings. Approach him and greet him again. You can make a mental offering of your choice in order to appease the god.

While going further, you can see a lake of boiling water, from which project the heads of those who are being boiled therein. You can see them and hear their weeping while passing by.

On the other side you can see a serpent, named Ankhaapau, who lives upon its own fire. You also pass a group of demons who destroy the dead and consume their bodies by the flames breathed out of their mouths. They have special blocks on which they cut the dead in pieces. In the meantime they sing hymns to their god, to the accompaniment of the shaking of sistrum. There is also a goddess (Qetet-Tent), who lives on the blood of the dead and sometimes also feeds on what gods give to her.

Around you can see the realm of fire, pain and suffering: people cast into a lake of liquid fire, others tortured in boiling water or cut to pieces and then consumed by fire. There is no place for good and righteous souls here. There is only destruction and mutilation. Demons, serpents, and other enemy creatures approach you, each of them assuming the shape of your own memories of pain and suffering.

You are now standing before a tomb by which you can see two small birds weeping and shedding tears. It is the tomb of Osiris. Weeping together with them, you begin to feel relief. Pain and suffering are relieved and your soul is purified. You can now continue the journey and descend to the abode of Seker himself.

You walk toward a pyramid with the apex in the form of the head of the goddess (Isis). The pyramid opens and you are allowed the passage. Inside you can see an elongated ellipse, enclosed by a wall of sand. It rests upon the backs of two man-headed sphinxes. Speak the name of Seker and invoke the god to show you his presence. Then you will see how the eclipse opens and the image of the god is revealed. He has a human body, but the head of a hawk. He stands between a pair of wings of the great two-headed serpent. There is darkness everywhere, but the eyes of the god flash with a bright light.

You approach and merge your consciousness with the god's. You can feel now the divine power flowing through your body and mind. It is the divine creative energy from which the sun traveling through the Duat draws its power and ability to become reborn in a new, young form when it rises in the east at dawn.

In front of you appears the beetle of Khephra. It slowly guides you up, toward the way out. While ascending, you slowly return to your normal consciousness.

Open your eyes and close the meditation.

The Summoning of Set

Various Authors

The ritual was inspired by descriptions of Set from
Hermetic Magic by Stephen Flowers.

***

Calling forth the elemental powers:

Facing East, envision a winged serpent rising over the
horizon and say the name: **ERBETH**

Then, facing North, envision an infant child sitting on a
lotus blossom and say: **SESENGENBARPHARANGES**

Then, facing West, visualize a crocodile emerging from the
waters, with a tail in the shape of a serpent and say:
ABLANATHANALBA

Then, turning to the South, envision a falcon with its wings
outstretched and say: **LERTHEXANAX**

Finally, envision yourself enveloped in a cool flame. From
your feet the phoenix rises to your head, and fills you up
with power.

Invocation:

I invoke you, the Adversary of Order!
Lord of the Crimson Desert and Wastelands of Chaos!
I summon the god of the ocean's depths,
I raise Leviathan through this call!
Mighty Typhon of storms and changes,
I call you!

Through the words of Set
My will shall manifest in this world
I create my reality
I shape my desire
My will shall manifest through this calling!

I invoke you through the names:

SETH, SET, SETI, SETESH, SETECH, SETEKH, SUTEKH,
ERBETH, PAKEREBETH, BOLCHOSETH I
ATHEREBERSETH

I am he who was and shall always be.
My essence shall exist in Chaos and Darkness for eternity.
Through the Dark I shall emerge into the Light.

ABRAOTH, ATHOREBALO, KOLCHOI TONTONON!

Focus now on the power of Set, lord of the Crimson Desert, the Adversary, the essence of the Left Hand Path. He is the initiator of self-deification, the one who shatters illusions and reveals the true nature of the world. Set is the lord of dreaming nightmares, and the one who challenges the magician. Only the passing of his tests allows for strength and progress on the spiritual path.

The Desert of Set
Meditation

Various Authors

Visualize yourself in the middle of the great desert. The desert stretches so far that you cannot see anything but the sand and the red sun above. The red sunlight creates an impression that the desert sand is of the same blood-red color. You go straight forth, but still you cannot see anything apart from the burning sun that scorches your body. You seem to notice vague shapes of shadows appearing from time to time around you, but it is not possible to take a closer look or even guess where they might have come from. The sun is burning the back of your body. You feel its heat flowing through your spine. In the distance you notice a hill. You go in this direction. From the top of the hill you can see a dark place beneath. It looks like a long forgotten burial ground. You realize that you are in an ancient graveyard. There are strange looking stones, behind which you can see shadows emerging and disappearing. Now they are clearer and more tangible. You go further into the burial ground.

Suddenly you hear a scream behind you. You turn around quickly and notice a figure standing in front of you – dark, shadowy, winged. The figure is holding in one hand a skull of a wolf, in another – a skull of a goat. You no longer feel the scorching heat. Now the cold northern wind flows through your body. You approach the figure, but it is fading and disappears. You are now standing at a place where the shadowy figure was a moment before. Suddenly the ground opens up beneath you and you fall down. The space above you closes. You are now in the underworld. It is dark in there, but your aura shines and lights it up. You go through a dark narrow path among serpents writhing around you as you walk. You sense the presence of shadows surrounding you, demonic entities. You feel their breath on your neck, and their claws scratching on the walls. Watch out so that none of them will hurt you and avoid being bitten by the snakes. If they attack, use magical fire – this will hold them back. Go straight ahead.

Now you enter a chamber where the judgment of the dead is taking place. In front of you there is a throne on which you notice a figure in a mask of a hawk. You approach the throne and look straight at this figure. The closer you are, the more changes are visible – the mask now transforms into a strange ass-like animal. Suddenly the figure rises. You are facing Set, the Lord of the Crimson Desert. His body is enveloped in fire, his hair shines with a red blaze. He takes off the mask and gazes straight into your eyes.

At this moment you feel surrounded by fire. Instead of Set, you see an enormous eye. You stand inside the eye. Inside and outside of you the fire is burning. Again, you find yourself in the desert. You feel unity with what surrounds you – the red sun, the fire, the desert sands. You *are* Set. At your command the sun disappears behind the horizon. The northern winds obey you. Yours is the rule over the night and the dawn. Focus on this feeling and slowly get back to normal consciousness.

The Soul in Ancient Egypt

Asenath Mason

While describing the ancient Egyptian concept of the soul, there are usually three important spiritual qualities enumerated: *Ka*, *Ba*, and *Ach*. The ancient Egyptians, however, believed that the human being consists of nine different elements. These were:

Khat **(Kha)** – the physical form. The mortal flesh of man which undergoes death and decay. It could be preserved only by the process of mummification.

Ka – the subtle body. The energy of each living being, which does not die and lingers even after the death of the physical body. *Ka* was the vital force underlying the life instinct, and also performed protective functions. Originally, it was viewed as male in nature (the male fertility), and for this reason it was depicted in the shape of a bull. Later it became associated with spiritual functions, and its iconographic depiction were two arms pointed upward. Sometimes they rested on an ensign, which pointed at the divine qualities of *Ka*, as the ensign was the attribute of gods. Worn as an amulet, the image was to protect the owner from evil powers. The *Ka* was also associated with the vital energy generated by food, therefore it was essential to bring burial offerings to the dead (*kau*): instead of bringing material gifts, passers-by were asked to read aloud special magical formulas which allowed for "making the food alive" with the power of the voice. There was also a special group of priests, called the servants of *Ka*, whose task was to bring ritual offerings to the dead thrice a day. This part of the soul was usually revealed no earlier than after death. An exception to this rule was ascribed to pharaohs, who were viewed as divine beings, close to the sphere of sacrum. It was believed that in their case the *Ka* manifested already in life. It was also thought that *Ka* could manifest in each living being under the influence of certain magical practices. The word *kau*, the plural of *ka*, also meant "offerings" or "embodiments." These were: force, strength, creative will, nobility, stability, light, knowledge, magical intelligence, taste, sight, hearing, nurturing, abundance and longevity. *Ka* was born together with man, which was depicted in numerous images in which the god Chnum creates a child on the potter's wheel, and together with the child he also makes its spiritual double – *Ka*. After death, the *Ka* remained in the tomb of the deceased and inhabited their mummified bodies or statues which represented them. It could move, eat, and drink, and in order to "live," it needed material food, just like before death. *Ka* represented both the higher, protective force, and the basic, mundane instincts related to the physical world.

Ba – the actual "soul," "psyche" of man, the vital essence. It was presented as a black swan or a bird with a human head. During the day it remained in the tomb of the dead and provided the air and the food. At night it travelled on the Solar Barque together with the god Ra. *Ba* did not need any food, as it fed on the Sacred Tree of the goddess Hathor and drank the water of life from the sacred pool. In old religious texts, *Ba* was the term which referred to the new deities who had no name yet. Later it was also the word for a single divine power. These deities usually consisted of many *ba*, depending on the function which they performed. It was also the name for the outer form of a god, e.g. Apis in Memphis was worshipped as "ba" of

Osiris. It was only at the dawn of the Old Kingdom that *Ba* became viewed as the immortal spiritual power of man.

Khu (*Akhu, Ikhu, Akh, Ach*) – the intellect. This spiritual quality was associated with the human mind. Like *Ba* and *Ka*, it was immortal. It represented not only intellect but also the will and intention of man, which existed even after death and ascended to the heavens in order to live there together with gods and stars. *Khu* manifested after the judgment which every dead person had to undergo, and after his *Ba* and *Ka* united. Originally, *Khu* was ascribed only to gods and kings – it marked a pharaoh as the divine son of Ra, the embodiment of power, strength, and the divine light in man. In the New Kingdom period it was acknowledged that common mortals also possessed *Khu*. In Egyptian iconography it was depicted as an Ibis with rainbow-colored feathers. It represented spiritual transformation into the highest spiritual principle which occurred after death. In one of the Pyramid Texts we read: "*ach* belongs to the heaven, and the body belongs to the earth."

Ab (*Yb, Ib*) – the awareness of feelings and emotions. In the human body, this spiritual principle was represented by the heart, the center of feelings, good and evil. *Ab* also expressed moral consciousness. It was the mediator in the conflict between the individual will and ties into the surroundings. The function of Ab was to balance the contradictory spiritual drives within a person and to maintain the inner harmony. After death it could leave the body and live together with gods, or it was devoured by Ammit (the monster which lurked by the scales of judgment to consume those who were evil in life), if this was the sentence in the hall of Maat.

Sekhem – the will of creation. A formless life-force of man, which existed together with Khu in the heavens after a person's death.

Khaibit – the shadow. In tomb paintings from the New Kingdom period, we often encounter a black shadow, the part of man which leaves the tomb together with the soul. The shadow had a protective function and its iconographic depiction was the fan. Sometimes the term *Khaibit* was referred to as an image or the whole appearance of a person, and sometimes it was identified with the physical body or the corpse. It was believed that the shadow could detach itself from the body, but it usually stayed close to *Ba*.

Ren – the true name, also the magical name which represented the Higher Self of a person. *Ren* was the vital force and magical power. It was believed that a person can be destroyed or endowed with power by someone who knew their *Ren*, true name. Therefore, Egyptian ceremonies of giving the name were held in secret and the true name was often hidden behind a pseudonym.

Sahu – the incorruptible spiritual body of man. It manifested after the judgment in the hall of Maat. Then it appeared from the physical body, preserving all mental and spiritual qualities of a person.

Apart from these elements, a significant spiritual element was *heka*, magical power. It was believed that in the human body it resides in the stomach. *Heka* performed an important function both in life and after death: it was the force by which the creator god Atum-Ra created cosmos. It was personified as the god Heka, without whom the other gods could not exist. It was the "First Work," also called Khunum in the Egyptian pantheon. *Heka* was the spiritual power on which the whole creation was founded, and it was the human will-power at the same time.

According to ancient Egyptian beliefs, not only humans but also animals possessed a soul – their own *Ka*. Apart from them – also plants, water, stones and other elements of nature. It is significant that the soul was inseparably connected with the body. That is why it was so important to preserve its physical vessel after death, in possibly the same condition as in life, because also then it was supposed to contain the soul.

Bibliography:

1. Ada Russo Pavan: *Tajemna wiedza Egiptu*
2. Stephen Edred Flowers: *Hermetic Magic*
3. Manfred Lurker: *Gods and Symbols of Ancient Egypt*

Exploring the Mystery of Sirius
The Bright Isis and the Dark Nephthys

Adam

"The soul of Isis is called Dog by the Greeks."
Plutarch

Sothis is the ancient name of the star Sirius, attributed by the Greeks. In Egypt it was significant that the entire calendar was based on its cycle, and the first appearance of the Dog Star on the eastern horizon (its heliacal rising) marked the beginning of the new year. This phenomenon was of an enormous significance for ancient Egyptians who built their monumental temples so that they would face the horizon into the direction of Sirius rising. An example of such a sanctuary is the temple of Isis in Dendera – the ancients believed the Dog Star to be the soul of Isis. And like Osiris was the consort of the Queen of Gods, so the companion of Sothis on the night sky was the star Orion. Sirius itself was called by the Egyptians Sept, while Orion bore the title Sah. The etymology of the title "Dog Star" is quite ambiguous and complex, and associations with the divine figures stretch back to ancient Sumer, through Egypt, until the times of Rome. In Greek mythology, for instance, the star was believed to had been placed in the sky by Zeus, the dog being the faithful companion of the great hunter Orion.

But before we proceed to further discussion, it is essential to mention the basic facts and the history of this mysterious star, and to be more specific: a group of stars. Sothis, which is located in the "Greater Dog" constellation, is the brightest star in the night-sky. It is a binary star which consists of blue-white main sequence dwarf star (Sirius A) and a faint white dwarf companion (Sirius B). Sirius B is enormously hot and its radiation is much stronger than that of the Sun. The temperature of this star exceeds 10.000 degrees. However, its size makes it "so dark" that it emits not much light. Some apparent orbital irregularities in Sirius A and B also imply the existence of Sirius C. This has not been confirmed yet, but scholars seem to support this theory. What is interesting, Isis as Sirius was depicted by the Egyptians in a barque with two companions. Perhaps they represented Sirius B and C. Ancient astronomy may seem primitive to a modern man, but in fact the ancients had quite specific and broad knowledge about the star in question.

While discussing the role of Sothis, it is essential to mention the Dogon tribe from Mali who knew about the existence of Sirius B thousands of years before modern astronomers made this observation in 1862. They were also in possession of other detailed information, such as e.g. the orbital length of Sirius B around Sirius A, which is fifty years. It is also worth noting that they claimed the existence of another star near Sirius. They called it Emme Ya (meaning: "sun of women"). For further information on this subject I recommend the famous book by Robert Temple: *The Sirius Mystery*.

Getting back to the main subject of this essay, let us discuss the association of the main Egyptian goddess with this most mysterious star of the ages. Isis herself perfectly fits the Mother Goddess archetype. She is the daughter of Nut and Geb, sister of Set, Nephthys, and Osiris, and mother of Horus. She was often identified with Athene, Selene, Tethys, or Persephone, and her cult might be traced even further. As the consort of the main god in the pantheon, she rules with him over the earthly kingdom. She is the mother and the queen, with such attributes as fertility and maternity. This is also linked with Sirius itself which was rising at the time of the Nile flooding. The water fertilized the barren earth and brought crops and abundance to the people. The Egyptians, however, believed that Sirius itself was the source of vital emanations. Isis is also the friend of the dead. As we can read in *The Book of the Dead*, she is the giver of life and food to the dead. She can also be one of the judges who measure the worth of human souls after death. She is depicted with wings spread, which was the sign of protection over the dead. It was her who conducted the burial ceremony of her husband after he was murdered by Set. Isis was also worshipped as the ruler of magic. She could treat diseases with herbs and send healing dreams to a suffering person. She united opposing principles: birth and burial, life and death. Hence we can conclude that the key to her nature might be found in exploration of these mysteries.

Just as the companion of Sothis is Sirius B, so the dark counterpart of Isis is her dark sister Nephthys. While Isis represents birth, growth and vitality, her sister stands for death, decay and stagnation. She is the darkness complementary to the light of the Queen of Gods. While Isis is the day, Nephthys is the night. She is the bareness of the desert, opposed to the fertility of nature. Once again we encounter a theory that the ancients interpreted all this in a symbolic and literal way. Even though the rising of Sothis, as we have already mentioned, was associated with the life-giving overflowings of the Nile, these days were at the same time the hardest and the most deadly in the year. This was because of extremely high temperatures at the summer solstice. In the literal sense, the Egyptians believed that the soul of a deceased person goes to Nephthys and to the heavenly barque. When the dead visit Nephthys, their "double" (ka) is written in the sky and immediately starts to rotate like the Sun. At this time it proceeds to the Duat (the Egyptian underworld) and is the pure life on the horizon as Sah (Orion) and Sept (Sirius). It was therefore thought that the stars were originally the houses of the dead souls.

In order to gain deeper insight into the mysterious nature of Isis and Nephthys, we will analyze the role of two deities to which they are both related: Anubis and Osiris. The myth of Nephthys and Osiris describes how she assumed the shape of her sister by a magic spell, got Osiris drunk on wine and seduced him. From this union she gave birth to Anubis. He was depicted as a man with the head of a jackal or as a black dog accompanying Isis. Anubis was the god of the dead and mummification. Therefore, if we associate him with the "Dog Star," we might come to certain conclusions. Plutarch writes: "By Anubis they understand the horizontal circle which divides the invisible part of the world, which they call Nephthys, from the visible, to which they give the name of Isis; and as this circle equally touches upon the confines of both light and darkness, it may be looked upon as common to them both." Again we might try to analyze this theory in a literal way, that is – correlating with the astral phenomena associated with the star Sirius, or in a more symbolic and metaphysical way. In the first case, the circle of Anubis could refer to the orbit of Sirius B around Sirius A, which circles around and guards it as a dog. As the god of death and the underworld, meaning the hidden, he might also be linked to the supposed third star of Sirius C. If we take a closer look at the metaphysical meaning of the circle symbol and refer it to Anubis, several theories might be put forward. On the one hand, the circle could represent the wholeness – elements of light and death united, which is represented by Sirius A and B united in the same group. This would also symbolize the harmony between them, as each element of this universum would be located at the same distance from the center. By the orbit we might mean the conception of time and cycle. What is interesting, the mummification process, the patron of which was Anubis, usually took seventy-two days, which is exactly the same time as the "journey" of the star Sothis through the underworld kingdom of Duat, i.e. behind the visible horizon. This could again refer to the concept of wholeness, as Anubis would guide the adept through the whole and symbolic period of death. "Time" in most mythologies is what gives birth to everything, but also to which all returns. On the other hand, as we can read in the above-mentioned quotation, as the intermediary between light and death, Anubis might illustrate transgression beyond the barrier of eternity and mastery over this process. Moreover, Plutarch also gives a Persian description of the Dog Star which is reputedly surrounded by fifty gods who constitute the shape of an egg (an ellipse) on which the "gods of light" oppose the "gods of darkness" – which is the symbol of wholeness, as well as the core of being. In this case, the role of Anubis as the psychopomp allows for interpretation of the circle as a form of a symbolic gate to the world of darkness and the unknown. Considering his mercurial/active nature, this period would stand for the journey into the underworld and resurrection.

Perhaps some additional light can be shed by the analysis of Isis' husband, Osiris. The Egyptian papyrus calls him "Lord in the perfect black," and the Trismegistic text called *Virgin of the World* refers to "The Black Ritual" connected with the "black" Osiris as the highest stage of initiation: the ultimate mysteries of Isis. As Robert Temple writes, "the Black Ritual" probably referred to the concept of the Night which was an object moving in the sky together with other mysteries which orbited in a harmonic way. It reputedly had less light than the Sun and "wove the web with fast light," which suggests a correspondence to the mysteries of Sirius B. But what further sense can this have?

In ancient Egypt the black color (khem) was the symbol of death and night. Osiris, the lord of the underworld, was also called the black god. Deities of necropolis and death, such as Anubis, were also connected with this color. But black in Egypt also meant life and resurrection because of the color of fertile mud near the Nile. In darkness humans died and were transformed to new life after death. In this sense the black color refers to the concept of immortality and transgression beyond dualities. What is also interesting is that the Egyptian sign "tchet" (snake) has two meanings: "snake" and "flesh," as well as the sign "ara" which represents a cobra: "snake" and "the goddess." Probably for this reason the Greeks presented Sirius with the symbolism of the snake, which is an obvious representation of eternity and immortality.

More information might be found in the analysis of the name, and more specifically: the transcription of the name Osiris. The oldest and simplest form of this transcription consists of two hieroglyphs, from which the first depicts a throne and the other an eye. This would translate the name as "the throne of the eye" (what is curious, the Bozo tribe in Mali, Dogon's cousins, describe Sirius B as the "Eye Star"). The name of the goddess Isis probably means "the throne," and in the astral sphere her counterpart is Sirius. The word "Osiris" might also be a misspelled transcription of the Egyptian name "Asar" or "Usar." This could also mean "The Eye Power" or "The One Who Sees the Throne." On the one hand, this implies a person who sees the true nature of the star Sothis which has a dark, invisible companion, both in a metaphorical and literal sense. On the other hand, if we compare it to another title of the Black God, we can draw even more surprising conclusions. The world "hen" means "to behave like a beast," and the word "henti" - "a person like beast." Henti is one of Osiris' names, as well as the animal which is an archetypal companion in legends about the Dog Star. Another title of

Osiris was "Unnefer," deriving from the root "ur" – "open, appear, create, and manifest." When we gather all these facts together, we might suggest a theory that the Black Ritual, which was the greatest mystery of the cult of Isis and Sothis, referred to the one who is aware of both sides of the universe: the bright and the dark one, and through the exploration of the unknown, on the path of the beast, creates oneself out of the new universe. What is significant is that the symbols of the eye and the throne correspond to the last initiatory level on the Tree of Night, the Thaumiel Qlipha: the place where the magician becomes an absolute root, the Eye of the Dragon and the Throne of Lucifer. And in fact, it is the place of the ultimate mystery which is to lead an adept to creation of a completely new world.

According to ancient Egyptians, Sirius and Orion radiated emanations which gave life to gods, humans, and animals, the creatures which arise from the seed of the soul. They believed that the seed which gives energy to the world emanates from the Sirius system. The seed is the symbol of the very center of existence, just like a point/circle/root or core. It contains all potentiality and creative activity. Of course, this essay is mostly speculative, and many clues suggested here are aimed at encouraging the reader to carry on their own research into this matter. The Sothis mystery, as we have already noticed, refers to the most important goals of the Left Hand Path – reaching to the root of existence, uniting the light and darkness within and outside, and acquiring the power by which a magician can become the creator of their own universe: a kind of a closed space, which is active eternally and maintains the unlimited potentiality. These are the mysteries which transgress beyond the boundaries of time, death, and doubt – so that we can rise and cast the bright red light through the vast recesses of space – just as the Sothis star during its heliacal rising.

Invocation of Nephthys

Various Authors

Light black candles and burn strong incense. Put a chosen depiction of the goddess on the altar. When you feel ready, begin the invocation:

We summon Nephthys, Mistress of the House in the sky!
We call you, daughter of Nut and Geb, child of the heaven
and the earth!
Friend of the dead and protector of the living!
Lady of the air and the rain!
Wife of Set and mother of Anubis!
Sister of Isis and lady of the dark moon!
Nephthys! Nebet-het! Nebt-het!
Come to us and answer our calling!

We wish to unite with your essence!
Come and fill our souls and minds with power and vision
of eternal mysteries!
Guide us to your temple and reveal to us the secret of
power which allows for creation and destruction!
Transform us through your force of the Dark Moon!

Nephthys! Dark Isis! Mistress of the Temple!
Come forth at our calling!

Ho Drakon Ho Megas!

Meditation

Sit comfortably or lie down. Relax and begin the visualization.

Visualize the full face of the moon above you. Breathe slowly and deeply, and envision that the air which is flowing into your body makes it lighter. You rise above your physical flesh and float up, toward the bright, shining moon. You rise above your temple, over your town, and finally leave the whole earth behind, slowly drifting toward the moon.

While approaching the moon, you notice that it slowly turns around and is no longer bright. It turns to the other side. Instead of the bright light, now you can see the black and pulsating surface. Suddenly a black bird, a hawk, appears before you and flies toward the black moon. You follow the bird and fly after him toward the dark surface.

You land on a completely black earth. There is nothing around, but in the distance you notice a black stone building, a temple into which flies the hawk who has led you here. Again, you follow him and enter the temple.

You can feel a shivering cold, even though there are lots of torches around. The fire is dark and does not give much warmth or light. Inside the temple it is quite dark. You can smell the scent of blood and you can see sacrificial bowls filled with this liquid, still warm.

In front of you there is a stone altar on which you can see the ritual tools and a statue of a hawk made from black stone. Speak the name of the goddess. At this moment the statue becomes alive and starts to grow until it becomes a huge shadow which devours you.

Let the goddess' power fill your mind and open yourself for visions. When they end, return to your normal consciousness and open your eyes.

Sacred Sexuality
Eros and Religion in Ancient Egypt

Asenath Mason

In ancient Egypt, sexuality was regarded as an everyday aspect of life and sexual issues were never considered a taboo. This was reflected not only in the life of people but also in myths of the contemporary deities and diverse religious customs. In the stories about the life of Egyptian gods we find many descriptions of their sexual life and erotic adventures, which apart from common matrimonial aspects, included also adultery, homosexuality, autoeroticism, incest, and even necrophilia. Women enjoyed a great deal of freedom and before marriage they could lead their sexual life in an open way. There were also many contraceptive methods. A great popularity gained the cult of fertility – in the procession celebrating the festival of the goddess Hathor the celebrants carried an image of the phallus (the symbol of Osiris) and the vessel filled with water (the symbol of Isis), representing the affirmation of fertility and the prolongation of life.

Circumcision was practiced as well. The sources even mention group ceremonies conducted for this purpose, e.g. among priests in the temples. As the concept of sin was unknown to the Egyptians living at those times, such practices probably served to maintain the hygiene, just as the shaving of the head and the whole body, widely popular among the priests.

Ancient Egyptians also knew many aphrodisiacs, the most popular of which was the lotus flower. Apart from the lotus, we can mention onion, lettuce, and mixtures of other ingredients: dill, ginger, pomegranates, and coriander mixed with honey.

Autoeroticism

The element of autoeroticism is already encountered in the myth of creation. As we find out from the story, the god Atum (sometimes identified with Ra) impregnates himself and gives birth to the first pair of gods: Shu and Tefnut. Atum himself is a personification of the primordial chaos from which everything was born. He arose by his own force himself and existed as the first god, before the sky and the earth were separated. He possesses the power of creation and destruction, which he reveals in conversation with Osiris, when he says that he will bring the world to an end and then he will assume the form of the primordial serpent once again. Atum is a hermaphrodite, "the great man-woman" who can impregnate himself and give birth. The first pair of deities which he creates is air and space (Shu) and moisture (Tefnut), sometimes referred to in sexual terms as the moist vulva of the female. It is often claimed that Atum created these two deities by masturbation, and his hand is considered the female element inherent in his nature. Atum and his hand are depicted on some sarcophagi from the Heracleopolitan period as a pair of gods. Another version of the myth tells us that Atum's semen was spitted or vomited by him, which suggests that he performed *autofellatio* by his own mouth. There is also another version, however, which claims that Shu and Tefnut were conceived in a sexual act of Atum and his shadow, which was referred to as *Iusaaset*, meaning "the great one who comes forth."

Androgyny is a widely known phenomenon among primordial deities in many mythologies. Egypt is not an exception. It represents the primordial nature of the god-creator who has no single gender in the act of creation and does not need a partner. The god Ptah of Memphis was also depicted as a figure of hermaphrodite nature – both male and female at the same time.

A similar deity was Hapi, the personification of the Nile. Originally he was an androgynous deity, closely related to the primeval ocean of Nun. Later he was depicted in male form but with female breasts: "He is the form of the Nile, one half of which is female, the other male." The goddess Mut of Thebes represented the full aspect of maternity, together with the role of fatherhood. One of her depictions even presents her with a phallus. Also the goddess Neith bears the title "father of fathers and mother of mothers." Isis herself, in the mysteries of Osiris, says "I became the man, even though I was a woman, so that your [i.e. Osiris] name lived on the earth." Finally, also the son of Horus, Imset was presented alternately as a male figure or one resembling a female, with no beard and with yellow skin.

Incest

Incest was often encountered in ancient Egypt, both in the myths of the gods and in the stories of kings and rulers. Among the gods we often find marriages between a brother and sister, starting from the first pair of deities: Shu and Tefnut. From their relationship another pair of gods was born: Nut (the personification of the sky) and Geb (the god of earth). And again, these two engaged in a constant state of love making. The legend has it that this aroused the anger of Ra, who ordered their father Shu to separate the lovers. And so it happened. Nut was raised up to the sky, away from Geb, and when it was clear that she was pregnant, Ra put a curse on her so that she would never be able to deliver her children on any month of the 360 day year. But Nut had one more lover, the god Thoth. He played draughts with the god of the moon and won one seventy-fifth part of each day. From these parts he created five additional days in the year so that Nut could evade the curse. The spell cast by Ra did not affect them, and she could give birth to her five children: Isis, Nephthys, Set, Osiris, and Horus the Elder. It was said that Osiris and Horus the Elder were the children of Ra, Isis – of Thoth, Set and Nephthys – of Geb. And again from these five gods another incestuous couples were formed: Osiris married his sister Isis, and Set took Nephthys for his wife.

The motif of incest is also revealed in the myth of Isis and Horus. According to the story, Isis interfered in the competition between Horus and Set. They both agreed to change into hippopotamuses and not to emerge out of the water for three months. Isis, however, worried about her son, whom she considered weaker than Set, and hit one of the animals with a harpoon. The wounded hippopotamus appeared to be Horus who had to go out of the water and lost the competition. In order to punish his mother, Horus raped her in a brutal way. This was to prove that he was as strong as Set and the judges could not claim the victory to his opponent.

Following the example of the gods (or the other way round), incest became the common tradition among the rulers of Egypt. The succession line was matriarchal and ran through the female representatives of the royal family. To become a pharaoh, a man had to marry the daughter of the king, that is his sister (or step sister) - hence the tradition of incestuous marriages among the members of the royal family.

Adultery

The most famous myth of adultery between gods is the story about the incestuous act which occurred between Nephthys and her brother Osiris. Once Nephthys decided to seduce her brother in order to conceive a child. As both she and her husband Set were sterile (both were the personification of the barren desert), Nephthys decided to try luck with her brother, who in turn, represented the life-giving fertility. For this purpose she got him drunk, took him to her bed, and then they two engaged in an intercourse. The plan worked fine and from this union Nephthys gave birth to Anubis, the child which later was to become the god of death and mummification. But Set found a garland of melilot flowers in the bedroom of his unfaithful wife and discovered what had happened. Since then he hated his brother and planned revenge and his death. In metaphorical terms, this myth is translated as the presentation of the overflowings of the Nile, which reached even the barren lands and made the plants grow in this part of the country.

However, adultery was not approved in ancient Egypt. A single woman could lead her sexual life freely, without any social disapproval, but adultery in a married couple was regarded a crime. There were even cases in which unfaithful wives were sentenced to death.

Necrophilia

Among Egyptian stories, accounts of necrophilia appear mostly in the myth of Osiris' death. When Set finally managed to murder his brother and cut his corpse into pieces, he scattered them around the whole country. Isis and other deities searched for these parts everywhere, and eventually she managed to gather the whole corpse together, with the exception of one piece – the phallus of her husband. It was eaten by a fish in the Nile, and thus, forever lost. Then she created another phallus, out of clay (depending on a myth this could also be wood or gold), and made it alive by her magical power. After that she breathed into the corpse of her husband enough life so that she could have sex with him. From this union she gave birth to Horus, their son. In order to celebrate this event, there were processions in which women walked through the streets singing and carrying statues with enlarged genitals. *Membrum vivum* of the dead Osiris was regarded as the symbol of vital powers which conquered death.

The belief in sexual life after death was also a common conviction among ancient Egyptians. For this reason mummies of dead men had artificial members attached, and those of women – false nipples, so that the dead could have sex also in the afterlife. Fertility dolls were put into graves: they usually depicted women with children. It was believed that by continuation of sexual intercourse with the spouse after death the deceased could "conceive" a new, reborn version of oneself.

As we learn from Herodotus, in the workshops where the mummification was performed necrophilia was a common plague. Therefore, the corpses of young girls were brought there by their families not earlier than on the third day after death. In the hot Egyptian climate the corpses were decaying very quickly, and the delay in mummification ensured the families that the body of their relative would not be defiled.

Homosexuality

The deity most often mentioned in this context is usually Set. According to stories, he had a lover, the god Ash, a minor deity considered to be a protector of tribes inhabiting the desert areas of today's Libya.

While discussing the homosexual inclinations of Set, however, it is essential to mention the myth about the contendings with his nephew Horus. After Osiris' death the gods had to decide who should take his place – Set, his brother, or Horus, his son. In the meantime, between these two arose a competition which included many homosexual adventures:

"Then Set said to Horus: 'Come, let us have a feast day at my house.' And Horus said to him: 'I will, I will.' Now when evening had come, a bed was prepared for them, and they lay down together. At night, Set let his member become stiff, and he inserted it between the thighs of Horus. And Horus placed his hand between his thighs and caught the semen of Set."

After that, Horus went to his mother, Isis, and told her what happened. She aroused him and he ejaculated to a jar. Then they spread Horus' semen on lettuce – the favorite vegetable of Set (the lettuce was considered an aphrodisiac by ancient Egyptians). When Set ate the lettuce with the semen, he became impregnated. When they both went to see the judges, Set was humiliated as the semen came out of him. This way Horus proved his sexual domination over his uncle.

There is also an earlier version of the myth, originating from ca 2000 BCE:

"The divine person of Seth said to the divine person of Horus: 'How beautiful are your buttocks, how vital! [...] Stretch out your legs ...' And the Person of Horus said: 'Watch out; I shall tell [this]!' Then he ran and told his mother Isis, that Seth desired to sodomize him. And she said to him: 'Beware! Do not approach him about it! When he mentions it to you another time, then you shall say to him: 'It is too painful for me entirely, as you are heavier than me. My strength [backside] shall not support your strength [erection]...' Then when he gives you his strength, place your fingers between your buttocks. ... Lo, he will enjoy it exceedingly. [Keep] this seed which has come forth ... without letting the sun see it..."

Then the story had a similar ending like in the previous version: Isis put Set's semen into the water, spread Horus' semen on the lettuce, and gave the lettuce to Set to eat. When later Set boasted to the gods that he had sexually taken Horus, the latter called forth the seed of both. The semen of Set answered from the water into which Isis had thrown it, while the seed of Horus came forth from Set's forehead in the form of a golden disk, which was grabbed by the moon god Thoth to become his symbol.

Generally, homosexuality in ancient Egypt was not viewed as negative. This is confirmed by the above-mentioned story. On the one hand it was considered humiliating to be abused by anal sex. It was a sign of weakness and disgrace for a man to leave his "proper sexual role" and allow for sodomy. The act of anal penetration was the symbol of power over the passive partner. Nevertheless, the contendings of Horus and Set brought positive results for Thoth. In one of the coffin texts we read: "Atum has no power over me, for I copulate between his buttocks," which suggests in a symbolic way that even the power of the gods could be limited. In *The Book of the Dead*, while enumerating all actions committed in life, the deceased declared (among others) that he did not sexually penetrate another male, had no sexual relations with a boy, and he did not defile his own body this way. Warnings against such actions are also found in the teachings of vizier Ptahhotep from ca 200 BCE. But even kings did not refrain from such relationships. Pharaoh Neferkare (Pepi II) was engaged in a homosexual relationship with his military commander, Saseneta (Sisene), who "amused the king" when there was no woman around. Akhenaten was suspected to have a romance with a boy named Smenkhkare. An archeological proof for the homosexual practices in ancient Egypt is also a tomb of two men named Niankhkhnum and Khnumhotep. They were found lying together, holding hands and embracing intimately. This way of burial suggested that their relationship was intended to last in the afterlife. Also the walls of the tomb contain many pictures and texts which reveal the nature of the relationship of the two buried men.

Ancient Egyptians were quite open and tolerant in regard to all sexual issues. If such a relationship occurred between two men, it was viewed by society in a neutral way. But if this concerned an adult man and a young boy, such relations were disapproved. It was not acceptable to tolerate a sexual relationship in which one side was evidently abused by the other.

Prostitution

Unlike in some ancient kingdoms, such as e.g. Mesopotamia, where we find the cult of Ishtar, in Egypt the phenomenon of sacral prostitution was almost absent. Nevertheless, in the Egyptian pantheon we can find the goddess of eroticism and sexual debauchery: Qadesh. Her cult spread to Egypt together with certain beliefs from the

Middle Eastern areas of Asia, which occurred during the New Kingdom period. The etymology of the name Qadesh might originate from *kedesh*, Palestinian temple prostitutes. She was most often depicted naked, standing on a lion, holding a snake in each hand. Sometimes she was identified with the goddess Hathor. Also this deity's characteristics pointed at her sexual nature: e.g. in her temple at Deir el Bahari there were many phalluses of wood and stone, which served as talismans providing fertility and allowing for child birth. Also the goddess Bast was associated with sexuality. In the late period she was considered the patroness of pregnant women, children, and all kinds of excesses, especially sexual.

Prostitution was commonly accepted in ancient Egypt. Prostitutes wore special garments, painted lips red and tattooed their breasts and thighs. Sometimes they walked completely naked. A custom similar to the Mesopotamian ones was practiced in the cult of Amun: a young girl went to his temple, had sex with whomever she wanted until menstruation. Then she returned home and got married. There are even theories that in the Karnak temple there was a harem with "concubines" of Amun. In fact, these women satisfied sexual needs of the priests, the earthly representatives of the god.

There are also controversial theories concerning prostitution as a part of the Hathor cult. According to these versions, young girls left home at the age of puberty in order to serve Hathor, the goddess of fertility. Then they became prostitutes until they gave birth to their first child. If the childbirth went fine and the infant was healthy and strong, such a woman had better chances to find a husband (in ancient Egypt women usually died at a very young age, often in childbirth). Then she returned to her family in order to get married. Hathor herself was not a chaste goddess. Among her lovers we may find e.g. Ra or the moon god Thoth. She was identified with the planet Venus and it was often observed how she "meets" other planets: Mars, Jupiter, or Saturn. In mythological sense, these "meetings" were viewed as relationships of a sexual nature.

Erotic Dancers

Hathor was also the goddess of dancing and music. Therefore, among her priestesses one could find many kinds of dancers. Erotic dancing often accompanied the fertility rituals and was the integral element of the sphere of sacrum. Hathor dancers from the Dendera temple were the most famous ones, but also other goddesses, like Isis, Bast, Sekhmet, or Nut, had their own ritual dancers. Dancing was the celebration of sexuality, life and rejuvenation. It represented the goddess and her powers – especially those related to the feminine element: fertility and sexuality. Couples who wanted a child travelled to the temple of Hathor in the belief that fertility rituals would help them in this matter.

But we also encounter erotic dancers in the wandering groups which visited towns in the time of religious festivities. Performing the role of the goddess, the girls danced, played musical instruments and sang. In the meantime, wine and beer was served – the most popular drinks of ancient Egypt. When the ceremony and its participants reached the peak of arousal, the dancers and male participants of the festivity joined in sexual union.

Other Gods of Sexuality

A typical symbol of sexuality was the god Min. In Egyptian art he was depicted in anthropomorphic form, with an erected phallus, holding a flail in his left hand, and wearing a crown with feathers. His attribute was the lettuce, which, as we have already observed, was a popular aphrodisiac. Lettuce was Min's sacrificial gift, representing the power of fertility that is the vital life force. In his festivities the processing celebrants carried the vegetable as his sign. His most significant festival was "the festival of the staircase," when he was presented the first ear of corns from the new harvest out of the hands of the king himself. This was symbolic of his function as the god of fertility, abundance and vegetation.

Another god of sexuality was Bes, a grotesque-looking dwarf-god, depicted with a giant phallus. He was believed to bring luck to married couples and their children, which associated him with the sphere of sexuality and childbirth. His image was often put in the so called *mammisi* (birth places). In Saqqara there were also "Bes-chambers" with walls lined with mud-plaster figures of Bes and a naked goddess. It has been suggested that pilgrims rested there in order to have healing dreams for their sexual or fertile powers.

There were also some other gods presented in ityphallic form and representing the power of fertility. Such are some of the depictions of Amon, one of them being a ram – another popular symbol of sexual potency. But Amon was also sometimes referred to as "Kamutef" (the same title was attributed to Min), meaning "bull of his mother," another animal representing the fertility powers. As a fertilizing male, the bull was the giver of the water of life, the one who brought the vital force. For this reason, the overflowings of the Nile were sometimes presented in a symbolic way in the shape of a bull. Rulers in the New Kingdom often had the title "the mighty bull," and sometimes the king himself was presented in this zoomorphic form. Another typical bestial symbol of male sexuality was the goat. There was even the cult of the goat in the town of Mendes. Women asked him for offspring, and the sacred goats were mummified after death.

The cult of Amon also included other practices related to sexuality. He was identified with the first creator of the universe (Atum), who performed the act of creation by masturbation. Therefore, in the temples one could find his depictions in which he was holding the phallus in his hand as the commemoration of the creation act. Behind a huge statue in the temple there was an entrance to a secret chamber, built for the royal couple. While performing the role of the god Geb and the goddess Nut, the king and the queen engaged in a sexual intercourse in order to reconstruct the second act of creation as it is described by the Egyptian mythology.

The Blood of Isis

This name was attributed in Egypt to a popular amulet, called also a *tyet*. It resembles the ankh, but its arms are curved down. The original meaning of the amulet is unknown, but there are many theories which link it with the concept of menstruation and female sexuality as represented by Isis:

"Egyptian pharaohs became divine by ingesting 'the blood of Isis,' a soma-like ambrosia called *sa*. Its hieroglyphic sign was the same as the sign of the vulva, a yonic loop like the one on the ankh or Cross of Life. Painted red, this loop signified the female genital and the Gate of Heaven. Amulets buried with the dead specifically prayed Isis to deify the deceased with her magic blood. A special amulet called the Tjet represented Isis' vulva and was formed of red substance - jasper, carnelian, red porcelain, red glass, or red wood. This amulet was said to carry the redeeming power of the blood of Isis." (Walker: *Encyclopedia of Myth and Secrets*).

Indeed, "the blood of Isis" was often put into graves as an amulet, and the temple walls were decorated with this symbol together with the Djed pillar. The association with the menstrual blood of Isis was made probably on the basis of the red color of the material it was made from.

Visual Arts

In paintings and temple decorations, sexuality is only slightly suggested, e.g. a husband and wife are sitting next to each other. Erotic scenes were presented with the use of metaphors and a particular kind of symbolism. The French scholar Philipe Derchain speculates that a mandrake berry might symbolize a voluptuous sensuality, or a duckling held between a woman's breasts might designate her function as a sexual partner. A commonly encountered scene from the tomb decorations (a husband and wife side by side to each other) represented their sexual union in the afterlife. In a similar way the contemporary artists presented the union between Isis and Osiris. They are never depicted in the act of sexual intercourse but rather with a subtle symbolism. Osiris is depicted in a human form, in the evident condition of sexual arousal. Isis floats over him in the form of a small bird which slowly descends toward the lying god. Such scenes are common in many temples from the New Kingdom period (1550 – 1070 BCE) and later.

A similar imagery was used to present relations between humans and anthropomorphic gods. Usually, they refer to the act of conceiving the king – in images his mother is impregnated by the god or his human father impregnates the goddess. Such depiction are found in the temple of the queen Hatshepsut (1478-1458 BCE) at Deir el Bahari, and also in the temple of Amenhotep III (1390-1353 BCE). They represent the god Amun-Ra and human queens who gave birth to Hatshepsut and Amenhotep III. Also in this case the sexual union is only implied, even though it is explicit in the accompanying texts.

Another scene with the theme of conception of the future king is presented on a painting in a small chapel erected for the cult of King Nebhepetre Mentuhotep (2008-1957 BCE). This time the sexual act occurs between the goddess Hathor and a human king – the ruler's father. Again we can see here a very subtle implication with certain symbols: Hathor shakes a sistrum (a symbol of sexual arousal) in the temple cult, and the king awaits her while seated on a bed.

From visual depictions of contemporary erotica the most famous is probably the Turin papyrus, which includes a series of vignettes with scenes presenting a man and a woman in diverse sexual positions. The positions are varied and explicit – presented in a more pornographic than subtle way, and embrace a wide range of sexual practices, which provides us with a more complete view of ancient Egyptian approach to sexuality.

Bibliography:

Barbara Walker: *Encyclopedia of Myth and Secrets*
Bruce L. Gerig: *Homosexuality in Ancient Egypt*
Budge, E.A. Wallis: *The Book of the Dead*
Griffiths, J. Gwyn: *The Conflict of Horus and Seth*
Manniche, Lise: *Sexual Life in Ancient Egypt*
Manfred Lurker: *Gods and Symbols of Ancient Egypt*
David O'Connor: *Eros in Egypt*
Caroline Seawright: *Ancient Egyptian Sexuality*
Jadwiga Lipińska, Marek Marciniak: *Mitologia starożytnego Egiptu*
Andrzej Niwiński: *Mity i symbole starożytnego Egiptu*

Bast and Sekhmet
Two Faces of the Feminine

Pairika-Eva Borowska

Life in ancient Egypt embraced a wide spectrum of religious practices, customs, and traditions. In this outlook, magic and religion were intertwined and inseparably connected with diverse aspects of everyday existence.

A commonplace man turned with his problems to the local deities, worshipped in the form of animals, rather than to the great gods of the Egyptian pantheon. It was believed that everyday work and life was at mercy of the Nome deity, and the local god could help or harm people, depending on the moral values which he or she represented. The Egyptian nobility, however, worshipped Ra as the main god, while all other deities, such as Set, Horus, Ptah, Amon, etc., were viewed as his distinct emanations. This essay is devoted to the goddess Bast, and her other, fierce aspect, called by the Egyptians Sekhmet.

Among the most important religious centers were such towns as Heliopolis, Memphis, Hermopolis, or Bubastis (where Bast was worshipped in the form of the cat). Each of these cities had their own gods and religious ceremonies, but all of them employed both magic and religion.

Bastet

In the town of Bubastis, located in the Delta region of Lower Egypt Bast was worshipped as the cat-goddess, a less fierce form of the lion-goddess Sekhmet. Other goddesses with which she was identified were Ubasti, Ba en Aset (the soul of Aset), Pasht, Hathor, Tefnut, and like her son, she was called Chonsu, and Mut, who in Greece was associated with Hera, Diana, or Artemis. Sometimes she was ascribed to the triad with the name Ptah-Bast-Nefertum. At the time of the Roman reign in Egypt, her cult spread to Italy, to Pompeii in particular. As it is known, her sacred animal was the cat, and in iconography she was depicted as a woman with a cat's head or in the form of a sitting cat. The word "cat" itself has many parallels in other languages and derives from the Egyptian word "utchat." Bastet was the mother of the lion god Maahes who bore the title "The Lord of the Massacre." For this reason, in the time of Bast festivities it was forbidden to hunt lions. She was the patroness of the joyful and cozy sphere of the domestic hearth, associated with love, nurture and protection. She was also the goddess of fertility and abundance - a protective mother, who was depicted with her offspring, but at the same time she could be fierce and threatening. Sometimes she was depicted holding a mask of a lioness, suggesting her hidden ferocity.

The cat in ancient Egypt was associated with the sun. It was believed that at night the god Ra travels through the underworld in his solar barque. During this journey he is threatened by evil spirits with the demon serpent Apophis as their leader. Lions were helping him by illuminating the way with their glowing eyes. As opponents of Apep, cats became sacred animals of the god Ra. They were believed to be one of his forms and became associated with the Eye of the Sun. Therefore, many cat statues were decorated with a scarab on their heads or chests. The scarab was obviously the symbol of the rising sun.

The attribute of Bast was the sistrum (a musical instrument), also often attributed to Hathor, whose elements were water and fire; red, green and white colors, and festivals in April and May. She was the goddess of the sun, but later, when she came to be identified with Hera, she became the moon goddess. In some sources she is mentioned as the daughter of Ra and the mother of Maahes and Chonsu. We can also find her in the myths as the daughter of Osiris and Isis, or as the twin sister to Horus. Sometimes she was viewed as the wife of Horus or Ra, and as Sekhmet – as the wife of Ptah. Each part of her body represented a similar part of the body of another god: the mouth – Atum, the nose – Thoth, the eyes – the Great Demiurge, the heart – Ptah, the belly – Osiris, the hips – Horus, the feet – Ra, and she herself was associated with the stomach. The whole cult of Bastet was abandoned ca 350 BCE and its ultimate end is dated to 390 CE, when it was legally forbidden.

Sekhmet: the Fierce Face of Bast

Sekhmet was the war goddess of Lower Egypt. Her name means "Powerful." Her husband was Ptah. She was always depicted as standing or sitting on a throne, in the form of a woman with a lion's head, often with a solar shield and the uraeus (a cobra symbol of royal power). Sometimes she also had a crown of ostrich feathers and the horns of a cow, like the goddess Hathor. Sekhmet held in her hand the sign of life, the Ankh, and the only garment she wore was the long, tightly fitted dress without sleeves, a broad necklace, and bracelets. Sometimes she was holding a staff in the shape of a lotus. Her festivals were celebrated on the 19th of November and 4th of December.

Sekhmet was another cat or lion goddess, just like Hathor, Bastet, Pakhet, Tefnut or Mut. She was also often identified with each of them, depending on the region. There was also a lion couple called Ruti, who represented the male and the female creative force, and protected offerings for the dead. The center of Sekhmet's cult was in Memphis, where she was worshipped with her husband Ptah and their son Nefertum. Such triads were common in ancient Egypt. Another one with which Sekhmet could be associated was the triad of Amon-Mut-Chonsu in Thebes, Mut being the equivalent of the lion goddess.

Ptah was the creator god whose attributes provided balance to the destructive aspects of Sekhmet, and their son Nefertum was the patron of beauty and healing. Like Hathor, Sekhmet – the goddess of diseases and war – was the personification of the Sun Eye and its disintegrating force. There is a tale according to which Sekhmet was originally an aspect of Hathor. She became the divine punisher when she tasted the blood of humans. She was aggressive and war-like, her anger brought plagues, and her breath was the fiery desert wind which brought doom onto the whole mankind. According to the myth, when humans lived on the earth together with the gods, they rebelled against Ra. The father of gods called all the deities together and following their advice, sent his Eye (Hathor) to the desert so that she could slay all mankind. She turned into a lion then and took the name Sekhmet. After that she came to the earth and all whom she saw she slew, rejoicing in slaughter and the taste of blood. When Ra saw the Nile running red with blood and the havoc which Hathor wreaked upon the earth, his heart stirred with pity for mankind and he ordered her to return. But the goddess refused and kept killing humans of her own accord. Then

Ra sent his messengers to the island of Abu (today's Elephantine) so that they would bring him a great store of the red ochre. He mixed it with beer so that it would look like blood and poured it onto the fields. When Sekhmet arrived there in the morning, she saw the beer and thought it was blood of those she slew. She drank it until she was completely drunk and could not kill any more. When she got sober, Ra managed to call her off.

There is another legend about Sekhmet's disobedience to her father, the myth of the Sun Eye. But here we see her as Tefnut-Bastet who fled to Nubia, taking all of her water and moisture with her (Tefnut was the personification of moisture). When she was absent in Egypt, the land dried and people began to die. In the meantime, in Nubia, Tefnut turned herself into a lioness and went on a killing spree in her anger at her father. Finally, Ra sent the god Thoth to bring her back. Thoth, in the form of a baboon, amused her with stories and tales, and managed to persuade her to come back. It is also worth to notice that when Sekhmet is appeased, she becomes a benevolent entity called Werethekau.

Because of her fierce qualities she became the protector of the pharaoh: as a statue, the lion guarded the entrance to the temple, and the entrance to the crypt was guarded by two lion heads of the god Aker. She was also personified as a royal scepter, and some healing qualities were ascribed to her as well. Priests, whose task was healing, often prayed to her so that she would help them destroy the demons of sickness with her destructive power. Therefore, she was also the patroness of physicians and threatened the allies of Set and Apophis. She dwelt in the deserts of the East and appeared at times of wars, on the battlefields, to rejoice in the bloodshed. She represented the destructive force of the sun.

Later on, she lost some of her fierce qualities and became identified with the consort of Amon. Her relative was the panther Mafdet, representing the eternal principle of the sun rising in the morning and devoured by a beast at dusk. The panther was also a symbol of the judicial authority of the king. Therefore, Mafdet represented the divine power of executions. She was depicted near gallows, and she was also a functionary in the Hall of Two Truths. Also Sekhmet was the divine punisher and the beast who devoured the sun.

Bast and Sekhmet, two similar and at the same time different goddesses, seem to represent principles connected with both life and death. We might even say that they both constitute the whole image of a woman: the woman who gives life and takes it back; the woman showing passion and danger; the nurturing mother and the ruthless murderer. In ancient Egypt, women could achieve a high position both in the mundane and divine life. A priestess could become the embodiment of the goddess whom she served while practicing both religious customs and magical ones.

Bibliography:

Heike Owusu: *Symbole Egiptu*
Andrzej Niwiński: *Bóstwa, kulty i rytuały starożytnego Egiptu*
Alfonso M. di Nola: *The Devil*
Jadwiga Lipińska, Marek Marciniak: *Mitologia starożytnego Egiptu*
Tadeusz Andrzejewski: *Dusze boga Re*
Zenon Kosiedowski: *Gdy słońce było bogiem*

Egyptian Serpent Deities

Morgiana & Asenath Mason

Ancient Egyptian lore is one of these mythologies in which serpent deities are most often encountered. There were many serpent gods, demons, and spirits – both benevolent and evil. The primordial gods, such as Amon or the Ogdoad, were depicted in a serpent form. Serpents such as Mehen protect the barque of the Sun God Ra on its journey through the underworld and help to defeat evil serpent demons such as Apep. In the underworld itself we encounter myriads of snake demons: some with wings, some with legs, some spitting fire, and some others armed with knives. They threaten the Sun God and try to stop or delay his passage to rebirth. But also in the underworld we find the ancient serpent encircling the world – the cosmic primordial source of all life in which the Sun God is reborn each night in order to proclaim his triumph over death when he rises at dawn. Here we find the most ancient image of the Ouroboros, the serpent biting its tail: the eternal symbol of cycles and primordial unity. He also protects the world from the destructive forces of chaos. Here the kings wore the serpent emblem (the Uraeus) as the symbol of royal power and divine authority, the infinite Eye of Ra. It was believed that this symbol was given to humans by the god Geb as the sign of kingship.

In this article we will briefly describe some of those numerous serpent figures from Egyptian mythology. Yet, much more can be said about them as most of these figures have a complex meaning, and their role in Egyptian myths, art, and general worldview is much broader.

Mehen

He is one of the lesser known serpent deities in Egyptian lore. His name means "the one who is coiled." His main function was to defend the god Ra and his Sun Boat against Apep during the night journey through the underworld. For this purpose he coiled around Apep or around Ra. His most important task is revealed in the seventh hour/division of the underworld. Here the serpent Apep swallows all the water on which the Sun Boat is floating and threatens the god. The boat, however, assumes the form of the huge black serpent Mehen in which it glides onward. In the meantime, the other defenders fight Apep and defeat him so that the Sun Boat may continue the journey.

Mehen was sometimes identified with another figure from the Egyptian pantheon – Set, whose original role was also to defend the Sun God. In this sense, he was depicted in a human form but with a snake's head, standing on the boat of Ra. In ancient Egypt the word "mehen" was also the name of a board game. It is unknown whether the game had anything to do with the deity. Despite of the fact that the game resembled the body of a coiled snake, it had no religious significance.

Mehen is a protective deity. Like the Ouroboros, who protects the universe from chaos, this serpent god encircles the center of the macrocosm, the sun, and protects it from destruction. Sometimes he was also depicted as a cobra, which suggests his relation to the Uraeus, symbol of divine power. It was believed that the cobra from the emblem protected the king by spitting fire on his enemies.

Wadjet

The goddess Wadjet was also known as Uto. She was a serpent deity, depicted most often as a cobra. Her name means "papyrus colored," which is a reference to the cobra's skin. Originally, she was the patroness of the city of the same name, Per-Wadjet, and later also the entire Lower Egypt. In Egyptian iconography, she was depicted as coiled upon the head of Ra, and her function (like in the case of Mehen) was also to protect the Sun God. In the tale of Horus from Behutet and the Winged Disc, Horus assumes the form of a disc and places two serpent goddesses (Wadjet and Nekhebet) by his side. Their role is to help him defeat his enemies. In *Legends of the Egyptian Gods* by E.A. Wallis Budge we read: "And he [Heru-Behutet] made the goddess Nekhebit and the goddess Uatchit to be with him in the form of serpents, so that they might make the Sebau (Set) fiends to quake in [all] their limbs (or bodies). Their boldness (i.e., subsided through the fear of him, they made no resistance whatsoever, and they died straightaway." While Wadjet was the patron of the Lower Egypt, Nekhbet held the same position in Upper Egypt. Together they were known as two ladies of the pharaoh. In an esoteric sense, they might represent two Kundalini forms: the serpents Ida and Pingala which flow on both sides of the Shushumna, representing the cold/lunar current and the hot/solar one.

The Uraeus symbol originated from the depictions of Wadjet. The old Egyptian word "wadjet" means "blue" and "human eye." That is why the goddess eventually became the Eye of Ra. As the protector and defender of Ra, she was the goddess of fire (fire-spitting serpent), and it was believed that she attacked with fire those who threatened her.

Apep

Apep was a demon of darkness and chaos, enemy of light and order of Ma'at. He was regarded to be the greatest and most dangerous opponent of Ra. Apep personified all evil in the Egyptian outlook. His depictions presented him as a serpent, crocodile or dragon. His most known titles were "Serpent from the Nile" and "Evil Lizard." From some of his descriptions we learn that he stretched 16 yards in length and his head was made of flint.

Apep could not step beyond the horizon (which also made him a chthonic deity), and so he could not attack Ra by day. He lurked behind the mountain of Bakhu where the sun was setting. In the fight with the Sun God, the Serpent used his magical gaze to hypnotize the deity. He wanted to crush the solar barque in his coils. Sometimes he appeared in assistance of two other deities – Sebau and Nak. When he somehow managed to stand on the earth, he evoked chaos: thunderstorms, earthquakes and other disasters. At the time of a solar eclipse it was believed that Apep managed to devour Ra. Of course, his defenders quickly slew the demon to release the Sun God from his jaws. However, each night Apep returned, as he had lived in the land of death before and could not be killed.

There are many legends and tales about this mythological figure. Many rituals were created to protect the world from his destructive actions. There was even a workbook on how to fight with Apep (*The Book of Overthrowing Apep*). In the legend of creation written on the papyrus from Der-al-Bahali there is a fragment called "Incantations Against Reptiles And Noxious Creatures" in which we read: "Get thee back, Apep, the enemy of Ra, thou winding serpent (...) Thy head shall be cut off, and the slaughter of thee shall be carried out. Thou shalt not lift up thy face, for his (i.e. Ra's) flame is in thy accursed soul. The spell of the scorpion-goddess Serq driveth back thy might. Stand still, stand still, and retreat through her spell (...) Horus uttereth a spell over thee, hours hacketh thee in pieces, he spitteth upon thee. Thou shalt not rise up towards heaven, but shalt totter downwards. O feeble one, without strength, cowardly, unable to fight, blind, without eyes, and with thine head turned upside down. Lift not up thy face. Get thee back quickly, and find not the way."

As a personification of the primordial chaos, Apep belonged to the sphere outside the world created and structured by gods. He was the darkness which existed outside the order of Ma'at. His defeat was the symbolic triumph of the forces of light and order over chaos and darkness. From the Draconian point of view, he is the Black Dragon, the force of Shadow and Death. An alchemical principle of dissolution. He attacks the Sun in the seventh hour of the Duat, which represents the turning-point in the alchemy of spiritual progress on the path of darkness. From this moment the adept achieves the power of self-rebirth. In the myth it is the most dangerous moment of the journey, and after confronting Apep, the solar barque encounters no more serious threats on its way.

The Ogdoad

It was a group of eight old Egyptian deities who preceded the creation of the world, according to a Hermopolitan myth. These were four male-female pairs which together represented the primal state of all things. These principles were: nu/Naunet – the primordial waters, Kuk/Kauket –

darkness, Amun/Amunet – the air or invisibility, Huh/Hauhet – eternity or infinite space. Male deities were depicted with frog's heads, female - in the form of serpents. Apart from the gender and the name ending (female ending with –t) these entities did not differ much from one another. They were regarded as two sides of the same principle. According to the myth, these forces were chaotic and unbalanced, which resulted in the arising of a new entity – the god Ra. There are two versions of this story, however. The original one tells us how from the primordial seas emerged the mound on which an egg containing Ra was laid by a celestial bird. In the other version, a lotus emerged from the waters as a bud, and when it opened its petals, it revealed the beetle, Khephra. As the aspect of Ra, Khephra represented the rising sun. Further from the myth we learn that the deity turns into a weeping boy whose tears form all the living creatures of the world.

The Ogdoad is only one of the examples in Egyptian mythology where the serpent(s) had a central role in the creation of the world. The others were e.g. Kematef and Irta, about whom we will speak later; the serpent Nehebkau, about whom little is known, or the serpent Sa-ta (which means "the son of earth"). Sa-ta was depicted as a serpent with a beard, standing on human legs. His image is often found in Egyptian sacral art. Many of these serpent deities are also depicted together with another significant cosmogonic emblem: the lotus. As we have already seen on the example of the Ogdoad, the lotus was closely related to the concept of creation and birth. It emerged from the primeval waters just like the sun rising from the darkness of the night. The god of the sun floating onto the surface of waters in a lotus bud was a common Egyptian symbol of birth/rebirth.

Renenutet

She was another cobra goddess, depicted as a woman with a serpent's head. She represented the act of giving the true name (Ren), one of the soul aspects. Her name referred to this action: "she who gives Ren." It was believed that the newborn "had Renenutet upon their shoulder from their first day." Her name might also be interpreted as a "nourishing snake." In this aspect she was regarded to be the goddess of fertility and abundance, and she was the wife of Sobek – the god who represented the annual flooding of the Nile. Her gaze was believed to have the power of slaughtering enemies. As the serpent goddess she was often identified with Wadjet, and eventually became one of her forms. She was also sometimes seen as identical with Thermutis, another nourishing serpent goddess.

Thermutis was depicted as a snake or a woman with a snake's head, viper's head, to be more specific. Isis in her vengeful form was often presented with a viper on her head. The name "Thermutis" means "deadly." On the other hand, she was a benevolent goddess – the patroness of harvest and abundance. People brought her wine as an offering.

Kematef

He was the primeval cosmic serpent/dragon. In Theban cosmogony, he was a form of Amon, the creator, who resided in Medinet Habu. His name might be translated as "the one who lived until his time." He emerged from the primeval waters at the dawn of time and gave birth to another serpent: Irta ("the one who created the earth"). Irta was the creator of the world and it was him who gave birth to the new generation of beings: eight serpents with Amon among them.

It was believed that he could rise from the dead by putting on his snake skin. The name Amon itself means "hidden one." He is related to the element of air and sometimes considered "the breath of life." In his serpent aspect he was believed to be the *Ba* of Osiris (*Ba* – the soul or the vital element which existed after the physical death of a person. It could perform the same actions as a living person. Depicted in the form of a bird with a human head). He was worshipped together with the Ogdoad and it was believed that he impregnated the primeval chaos. Kematef exists outside time and the universe. He is the one who will remain even when the world ceases to exist. Originally, he was the god of Upper Egypt and the patron of fertility. But his significance increased when his cult spread to Thebes. There he was regarded as the father of gods, preceding the Ogdoad, even though remaining a part of it. The kings thought that all victories were granted by Amon, which resulted in a great significance of his temples.

Kebechet

Kebechet was a serpent goddess associated with funerary ceremonies. She represented the embalming liquid and she was the daughter of Anubis, the god of death and mummification. Her name meant "cooling water," and for this reason she was often considered a deity of freshness and purification through water. It was believed that she washed the entrails of the dead and gave water to those who waited for the end of the mummification process. This process was essential to provide the Ka of a deceased (one of the parts of the soul, the spiritual double) with a physical vessel in which it could exist after death. In the Pyramid Texts we read: "The Goddess Kebechet, the daughter of Anubis, finds Pepi, and she goes to meet him with the four nemset vases. She refreshes the breast of the

Great God on the day of his watch, and she refreshes the breast of Pepi with life. She washes Pepi, she censes Pepi." In Egyptian temples, there were priests who had a special job as a part of the daily ritual: they purified the temple deity. They used incense to purify the air. The statue of the deity was carried out of the temple, washed, anointed with oils, dressed in white, green, red and blue clothes, and fed. The act of Kebechet washing Pepi seems to be related to these duties of the priests.

Set

The ancient god was originally a deity of the desert, the barren part of Egypt. The exact meaning of his name is unknown, but it is supposed that it could mean "the one who dazzles" or "pillar of stability." As the god of the desert, Set was related to sandstorms and caravans. Because of the extreme desert climate, he was considered a very powerful deity, one of the main gods in the entire pantheon. In one of the Pyramid Texts we read that the power of the king is the power of Set.

He was the patron of Lower Egypt where his cult had its main center. His name was also spelt Setesh and later Sutekh (the additional *sh* and *kh* denoted nobility). The word "desert" in Egyptian is "Tesherit," which is very close to the word "Tesher," meaning the red color. Because of this, Set came to be associated with all that was red – also with people with red hair. The Egyptians did not have hair in this color, so Set became the god of outlanders.

In iconography, he is depicted as an unknown animal or a Typhonic beast with a curved snout, square ears, forked tail, and canine body. It bears no resemblance to any known animal. There is a new theory which claims that the Set animal is a representation of *Mormyrus kannamae* (Nile

Mormyrid), a fish which resides in the waters near Kom Ombo, one of the sites where temples of Set were built.

When Lower Egypt was unified through the conquest of the lower half by the Upper, this was reflected in contemporary mythology. As the patron of Upper Egypt, Horus battled with Set for authority over the whole country. In this fight it is said that Set gouged out one of Horus' eyes, which explained why the moon is not as bright as the sun.

Set was also the defender of Ra during his journey through the underworld. Apart from being a powerful and dangerous deity, Set was also a benevolent god, sometimes representing sexual pleasure. He was invoked by men in order to improve potency. But when the tale of Osiris and Isis appeared, Set came to be considered as evil. He was accused of murdering Osiris and dismembering him so that he could not be resurrected.

The Greeks identified Set with Typhon. Set was the god of the midday sun which scorched everything and made earth barren. He was also a friend of the dead, like Anubis. It was believed that "Horus purifies and Set gives strength, and Set purifies and Horus gives strength, until the spine of the deceased person becomes the spine of the god." In other words, he endowed the body with strength so that it would endure the decay.

Set embodied the forces of chaos as opposed to the forces of natural order. For this reason he was also often identified with Apep. But in other myths he fought the serpent together with other gods who assisted the Sun God on his underworld journey. As the one who opposed Osiris, he was the symbol of fighting with stagnation. As the one who defeated Apep, he was an emblem of triumph over blind chaos. Thus he provided balance and cosmic harmony. In an esoteric sense, he might be considered the patron and initiator of the Left Hand Path. The act of killing Osiris marks the end of the old order. It is a symbolic challenge to patriarchal structures enforced by authority and tradition. It is the essence of the antinomian path of spiritual progression. One of Set's attributed names is Set-Heh, meaning "God of Infinite Future." This represents his function as the initiator of the path toward Infinity, the one who awakens the serpent's force within and lifts it to the stars so that man might become his own creator.

Conclusion

The cult of serpents, as well as other feared animals, was believed to appease them and allow for the access to their dark powers. As they usually represented a form of chaos (either creative like Kematef, or destructive like Apep), their force was viewed as the most powerful among all others. It had great protective powers and could destroy enemies. Also, it protected the deceased who travelled through the underworld. In Egyptian iconography we often find depictions of God-Creator in the form of the Great Serpent, sometimes with wings, legs and the human head. This serpent represents the eternal principles of death and birth, creation and destruction. The Great Serpent is the form of Atum, the creator god who gave birth to all other deities. He is eternal and infinite, as he is the one who existed before all creation, and he is the one who will remain after all creation is destroyed. The serpent is the beginning and the end of time. In an esoteric sense, it is the Kundalini energy, the great evolutionary force which is the drive of all life and the source of immorality.

Yatuk Dinoi
Black Magic in Ancient Persia

Yatus

Zoroastrianism

The cult of the Wise Lord, Ahura-Mazda, also called in Greek Oromazdes (Hellenized: Ohrmuzd, Ohrmazd) was a religion that flourished among Iranian tribes throughout nearly a thousand years. Written on the pages of the *Avesta* (sacred texts of Zarathushtra's religion), the beliefs derived from the earliest antiquity, from myths and legends older than the Iranian status of an independent community, stretching back to Indo-Iranian influences. The oldest accounts of the cult of the Wise Lord (Ahura – wise, Mazda – lord) are estimated to be at least 2500 years old and were left by those "whom he gave power: the Achaemenid kings."

In fact, the religious doctrine of Zarathushtra (7th century BCE) was not a new religion but rather a restored belief originating from older forms of Ohrmuzd cults (Mazdaism), and was a sort of "a compromise between ideology and teachings" that were incorporated into Zoroastrianism. The most important of these ideologies were Zurvanism and Manichaeism. The concepts of the origin of the universe differ in Zoroastrian myths and were shaped by the doctrine and thought around which a particular myth arose. One of the cosmologic versions in

Zurvanite doctrine describes the genesis in the following way: in the beginning there was only Zurvan, the infinite time. There was no sun and no moon that would measure the months, days and years. There was no earth and no sky. Nothing existed apart from Zurvan. But Zurvan desired an offspring. He prayed and made offerings until he finally conceived a child. He imagined his unborn child as pure light, majesty, beauty and such absolute goodness that man cannot comprehend. But the thought is always involuntarily accompanied by its adversary – thus he imagined also the opposite character: darkness, ugliness, and evil, and a shade of doubt appeared together with the faith of a bright essence of the unborn. Apart from love, there were also opposite emotions: reluctance and envy. And although these were only shadows of feelings and thought, they were strong enough to conceive another son, the opposite of the first, embodying all qualities that Zurvan rejected. The other son was dark and evil, hostile toward the first one, aggressive and full of hatred. Zurvan was unaware of carrying two sons in his womb. As all-embracing unity, he did not know the nature of division, he did not know that separation always results in two things, not in one. Therefore he promised his first-born son the rule over the universe. But it happened that the son who emerged first from Zurvan's womb was not the desired bright son, the Wise Lord Ohrmuzd, but the dark, hairy, foul, and full of hatred: the first to come was Ahriman.

This is one of the versions of the myth about the beginning of all things. Another, influenced by the Persian Manichaeism, claims that originally there was only Good and Evil, Light and Darkness, the two primordial spirits, unaware of each other's existence. These are, however, stories that lay at the foundation of the official religion of Old Persia – Zoroastrianism, the cult of the idealized Good Lord who embodied the infinite wisdom, goodness, and purity. This purity was worshipped by early Zoroastrian priests (the Magi) in the form of fire. This Old Persian religion represents what the Western Hermetic Tradition calls the Right Hand Path – where the worshipper is obedient to the official moral laws (created by the Wise Lord himself) and social rules that govern the whole community, and has to follow these regulations in order to deserve the mercy of God (salvation). This god is usually somewhere outside, high in abstract heavens, and the goal is to reunite with him after the death of the physical body.

It is significant that in this and other cultures, mythologies represent not only the gnosis (revelation) but also social changes occurring during those times. The Mazdaic and later Zoroastrian dualistic concept of the eternal struggle between the forces of Light and Darkness is a metaphor of the rising Persian statehood – the transition from the nomadic (Ahrimanic) tribal life into the settled agricultural system from which the first monarchic dynasties emerged. The dualistic Persian mythology also influenced many later religious doctrines such as Gnosticism (especially the Persian Manichaeism and Mandaism, or modern neo-Gnostic forms such as anthroposophy), the foundations of the Slavic mythology, and the dualism of the Christian doctrine. However, few researchers of the esoteric tradition are aware that in the Persian empire, apart from the bright religion of Ahura Mazda, there was also another cult: the antinomian form of the occult rebellion – Yatuk Dinoih, the religion of Ahriman.

Akht and Matigan-I Yosht-I Fryan

The oldest known accounts of Yatuk Dinoih (in Persian: witchcraft or sorcery) are derived from the Middle-Persian period, from the so-called *Pahlavi* script (etymologically:

"heroic"), dating to 330 BCE – 326 CE. It was the time of the Sassanid dynasty. This tale is known as *Matigan-I Yosht-I Fryan* and describes an evil sorcerer, Akht, who travelled from town to town and challenged holy men (sages) with riddles. If they gave a proper answer, Akht let them go and live. But if they failed, he killed them. Riddles were in the form of questions that no one could answer. This way he killed 900 megvas (holy men) and the same number of women. Finally, Akht came to the town of Frashno-Vazaran, which means "the town answering riddles," but even there no one could pass his test. However, there was a young man called Yoistha Fryan, a wise and holy person. He accepted the sorcerer's challenge and thus the great game of questions and answers began. Akht asked thirty-three questions and all of them are given in the *Pahlavi* text. The young wiseman answered all of them and asked the sorcerer three questions of his own. Then, the tale describes a horrible ending.

This story, however, has another meaning – an esoteric interpretation connected with the magical knowledge and techniques of old Yatukan sorcerers. Ervad Marzban Hathiram in his essay about Matigan-I Yosht-I Fryan observes that Akht's tests were not usual questions and the wisemen did not die in a conventional way. The sorcerer created them on the basis of the Staota: the law of vibrations. The Staota was put into a tight spool that was given (as a question) to the challenged person. When they tried to open the spool (answer the question), the force would kill them if they were not able to deal with the vibration (energy). Michael W. Ford in his writings on Persian magic explains this in a modern interpretation, claiming that the words (questions) were the "demonic mantras of power" that awakened the primeval magical knowledge (atavisms), the alphabet of desire, in the sorcerer's mind.

Akht himself (sometimes called Akht Jadu or Kabed-us-spae) in the symbolism of the Yatukan magic is very important: he was both "creator and member of Yatus-coven of nomadic demons and sorcerers who wandered around Persia and practiced sorcery," as well as the embodiment of demonic powers of Ahriman, his earthly avatar (in regard to the nature and the goal of Yatukan initiation). He was the first (in Persia) to succeed in isolating the consciousness from "the natural order" (self-deification) through the dark alchemical transmutation.

Ahriman, Yatuk Dinoih, and the Left Hand Path

Ahriman, or Angra Mainyu, in Zoroastrian mythology and demonology, is the spirit of darkness, prototype of what in the Western culture is referred to as the Prince of Darkness or the devil – embodiment of the ultimate evil. The Greeks and Romans knew him as Arimanus, and Herodotus compared him to the Greek *Kakodaimonos*, meaning: evil spirit. The name "Ahriman" itself means "devilish spirit," or simply "devil." He is the creator and the lord of Daevas – evil spirits, one of the most ancient archetypes of the Western demons (the example of which is Aeshma Daeva, the spirit of hatred and fury, who in the European lore became Asmodeus). But the "evil nature" of Ahriman results from the patriarchal perception and the view imposed by the solar religion and the state authorities. In fact, he is like many other dark deities such as the Arabic Iblis, the Egyptian Set, the Judaic Satan (Lucifer), or the Slavic Czernobog. He embodies the primordial darkness and chaos that preceded all creation. In the act of creation, chaos gives rise not only to light but to the whole structured universe. In many ancient mythologies, this act is symbolically depicted as a defeat of a primeval monster, the symbol of original chaos, usually presented as a serpent or dragon. Ahriman is a typical example of such a primordial monster. One of his most common forms was that of a black dragon (also a wolf, toad, or serpent) and like other similar deities, he was the spirit of death and the patron of sorcerers and witches.

The old Persian path of sorcery was unknown to the culture of the West for a long time. The tradition of Yatus (nomadic sorcerers and demons) is still one of the least known or understood religions. Yatuk Dinoih is in fact an ancient Left Hand Path system, originating from the area of what now constitutes Iran, and has much in common with the Typhonian/Draconian current. Similarly as the Egyptian Set, the godform of Ahriman in the symbolism of the Yatukan cults personifies the concept of the Adversary. It is the point in which an individual consciousness is awakened from "the sleep" and through antinomian rebellion challenges the imposed world structures. Like Set, he is the initiator, the symbol of darkness, chaos, and the lunar current – although this particular aspect is more evidently embodied by Az, the female counterpart of Ahriman. Az is the vampiric "queen of witches" and "mother of demons," the Persian equivalent of Lilith, Kali, or Hecate.

In all this ambiguity of the "Devilish Spirit," the most important is his symbolism of the self-deified consciousness. Ahriman represents the magician who achieved immortality through exploration of the Dark Side and found there the beautiful light of Promethean illumination – the divinity within – the Black Diamond.

For a deeper understanding of this subject, it is interesting to compare the nature of Ahriman and his hierarchy of Daevas by means of Qabalistic analogy. Ohrmuzd and his emanations, the Amesha Spenta, personify the bright side of the universe that can be compared to the Sephiroth on the Tree of Life, representing particular aspects of God (this is also the character and function of Ohrmuzd). However, as each Sephira has its dark counterpart, so each Amesha Spenta has its dark equivalent, the antithesis in the form of the main Daevas that emerged from Ahriman's nature in the process of creation. Like the Qabalistic Qliphoth, the Yatukan demons represent the inaccessible aspects of the universe and the dark side of consciousness. And like Qliphothic energies, the Daevas are the dynamic, chaotic, and destructive forces.

Apart from vampiric initiation, the essence of the Yatukan magic also involves goetic evocations and invocations that stretch far beyond the practices of *The Lesser Key of Solomon*. When the goetic magician stands in the circle, afraid of the conjured force, Yatus (the sorcerer) or Pairika (the witch) consciously strive for a complete union with the evoked Daevas, and the ultimate test of awakening is to enter the evocation circle without any protection. By means of dark magical practices and inner alchemy, the nomadic followers of this forgotten religion worked to become like Akhtya (the founder of this cult) from the old Persian legends, the immortal sorcerer, to become strong enough to "transform desires into flesh" and to control the surrounding reality. Thus, through the communion with the most terrifying demons in history, they acquired their skills and knowledge essential to achieve the divinity – just like Ahriman.

Yatukan Magic in Postmodernist Times

Postmodernism, or postmodernist movement, seems a suitable term to characterize the today's world-picture: the period in which the contact with the sphere of sacrum has been replaced by mass media and each "modern" magical system is based on volatile identity, panpsychism, and eclecticism. The Yatukan tradition has also succumbed to the impact of the modern occult thought that might be called Magical Pragmatism. Apart from old techniques rooted in Persian traditions, this system has incorporated elements of Aleister Crowley's Thelema, Austin Osman Spare's Zos Kia Kultus, and inspiration from works of Jake Stratton-Kent, John Whiteside Parsons, or Charles Pace. Here we can also find traces of the postmodern system of Chaos Magic. The Yatukan sorcery also develops by incorporating elements of necromancy and vampirism from other related paths: Egyptian magic, Palo Mayombe, or Santeria. All this, however, occurs through a very modern and effective system of pragmatic dark magic and spiritual alchemy.

Yatukan Ritual of the Black Dragon

Various Authors

Lord of Shadows! Essence of Darkness! I summon your black spirits! I seek union with the Shadow that is hidden in the abyss of my soul! May the ritual begin!

Lepaca Kliffoth!

Take a sword or dagger and point it in the four cardinal directions, speaking the following words:

South

Shaitan! Lord of the Desert and the burning sun! Set! Bringer of Storms and Fire! Let your essence enter this temple. Come forth from the utmost Darkness! Light your Black Flame on the altar of my soul! I invoke thee!

East

Lucifer! Morning Star! Bringer of Light and Illumination! Phosphorus! Let your spark of divinity blaze brighter than the light of the midday sun. Fill this temple with the Promethean fire and light the flame in the abyss of my existence! I invoke thee!

North

Belial! Angel of misrule! Belhor! Spirit of Earth and Darkness! Source of impurity! Father of lust and earthly pleasures! Enter this temple with your spirits of Darkness! Come forth from the North, the realm of cold. I invoke thee!

West

Leviathan! Great Serpent of the Sea! Rahab! Seven-headed Dragon of Chaos! Embrace me in your timeless coils. Rise forth from the depths of dark waters and fill this temple with the power that lies hidden deep in the nethermost abysses! I invoke thee!

May the infernal gates open and may the powers of the Above and the Below enter this ritual space to witness and empower this ceremony!

Envision portals opening from the four directions and from above and below. Visualize the dark powers entering the temple and filling it with a thick black energy. Vibrate the staota:

Nonasturma

Raise your wand and recite:

Spirit of Darkness, Angra Mainyu, I invoke you! I am the wanderer on the path of shadows on which I seek your presence and your guidance. Lift the veil of light that conceals the true nature of the world and let me become immortal in Darkness. Awaken me through your dark communion and let me taste the fruits of infernal ecstasy. Ahriman! The Black Dragon of Shadows! Fiendish Spirit!

Let your dark forces into my being and reveal to me your essence through your seven archfiends!

Continue visualizing the temple being filled with thick black smoke.

Indra! Lord of Apostasy! Daemon of Isolation! Enter my consciousness. Light the spark which I shall transform into fire of deification. The false gods will pass away to make way for those who seek divinity within!

Zairitsha! Spirit of immortal wisdom! Reveal to me infernal treasures of hidden knowledge! Unveil the ancient wisdom of dark sorcery!

Sauru! Demon of Disobedience! Essence of Rebellion! Give me the strength and perseverance to walk the harsh path of antinomian isolation! Let me follow the stream of Chaos that shall become my tool of dynamic progression!

Naonhaithya! Spirit of Discontent! Move the wheel of eternal progress! Do not let me rest in a mere content of stagnation, but set the wheel of changes into motion so that I can always gather fresh fruits of my work!

Taurvi! Daemon of deadly venom! Destroy the weakness with your poison! Annihilate lies and illusions around me! Awaken in me the hunger for knowledge that shall be transformed into power!

Aka Manah! Lord of isolated consciousness! Plant the seeds of divinity in my soul and let them grow in the utmost Darkness so that I may emerge from the abyss of ignorance as an avatar of the Black Dragon!

Aeshma Daeva! Demon of lust and anger! Wrath and Revenge! Violence, Conflict and War! Awaken in me the

*fury so that I may, like a tornado, destroy all obstacles in
the way that I have chosen!*

*Lords of the Flesh
Lords of the Mind
Let my Will be proclaimed through your actions!
Let my desire become flesh!*

Vibrate the staota of power:

Yatukisahla!

*I become the vessel of Darkness which I transform into the
divine fire. Dark becomes Light and on this forbidden path
I approach my own godhood. May the Black Flame
illuminate my being!*

While vibrating another staota feel how the invoked energy
is entering and transforming your consciousness:

Izzadraana!

Ho Drakon Ho Megas!

Comments:

This ritual summons the seven Daevas, seven archfiends of
Ahriman, the Black Dragon, and uses them as vehicles of
self-initiation in the process of self-deification that is the
goal and essence of the Left Hand Path. The staota
(vibrations) used in the ritual are derived from the grimoire
of Persian witchcraft *Yatuk Dinoih* (second edition) by
Michael W. Ford.

The End of All Flesh

Pairika-Eva Borowska

„After the primordial light was withdrawn there was created 'a membrane for the marrow,' a *k'lifah* husk or shell, and this *k'lifah* expanded and produced another, who was Lilith."

(*Zohar*)

Lilith is a dark form of the feminine archetype encountered in many mythologies, from Sumerian, Babylonian and Assyrian, to such cultures as Hebrew or Teutonic. Originally a night demon haunting both men and women at night and causing erotic dreams, throughout ages she has become a witch, vampire, hag, and personification of all that is viewed as evil, impure, dark, and feared. She is Adam's first wife and first female in the world. Later on, she becomes the wife of Samael the Devil and Ashmodai. She is the Queen of Sheba and Zemargad. In some sources it is Lilith who becomes the female of Leviathan. And finally, she is even the consort of God himself in the absence of Shekinah. Lilith's energy is that of the night, dark and fiery. She appears in dreams, ruling the first astral level on the Qabalistic Tree of Night, the Gamaliel Qlipha. She is the dark feminine aspect of the Self, the feminine transpersonal shadow – by men experienced as a seductive but violent and fatal succubus, by women as a dark shadow of the Self. The integration of Lilith into one's consciousness is a necessary step on the path toward psychological individuation, or in esoteric terms – to individual self-deification.

Lilith
John Collier, XIX century

Invocation

LEPACA LILITH!

I invoke you – who first opened your womb to a human male! Come to me!
Answer my calling and protect your Children of the Night!
Goddess of the Moon, whose shrieking moan tears the night apart,
Give me the power to satisfy my dreams and desires!

LILITH, IZORPO, KALI, AZ, ABIZO, ZAHRI, ARDAT LILI, NAAMAH

Oh, Lilith!
Spider Vampire! Look at me with your blood-red eyes
And illuminate the path of my existence!
Show me the threads of Truth, Time and Dreams
Reveal to me the pattern of destiny!

OPUN, AMA, LILITH, RUACH, GEBUN, NERTHUS, IPAKOL

Through the gate of ecstasy the Great Dragon will awaken
And you will ride him to tread the deceits and illusions of this world and restore the sacred union of opposites!
From the depths of my soul Darkness and Light will emerge in an infernal union!
The fallen Angel Samael is born!

BABALON, LILITH, NAAMAH, TYPHON, TIAMAT, AZ, LIROCHI

Impure Female, Alien Woman, Woman of Harlotry, Vixen Bogey, End of Day, End of All Flesh! Come to me!

HO DRAKON! HO MEGAS! x3

Meditation

Visualize that you are walking at night through a thick forest. Above you can see a pale moon and the silence around is only sometimes broken by the voice of an owl. Something grasps your leg and you fall on the ground. You can feel something moving underneath and you know it is a living creature. You are paralyzed with fear but after a while you move back and look at the ground where you were lying a moment before. From the ground arises a huge cobra. At first it assumes a normal size but it grows very quickly and after a while it is as big as a tree. While it is growing, a silver aura starts to surround it. You cannot take your eyes away from it. You are paralyzed again and you look into the reptile's eyes with growing fascination and excitement. Its jaws open and you can see its forked tongue touching you. The cobra is hissing and suddenly you realize that you can understand its language. You declare your magical name and speak the words of greeting: Ho Drakon Ho Megas!

With one quick move the cobra bites you in your forehead, in the place of the third eye. A hole in the ground opens underneath and you fall into a tunnel which leads to the bowels of the earth, in the depths of your consciousness. You do not have a physical body – while falling, it is torn apart by the claws of the dead and spectral wraiths. In front of you there is a blood-red light. You are drawn to this place. After a while you realize that it is a cave which is lit by the glow radiating from the giant blood-red ruby. It lies in the center of the cave and resembles a strange altar. You come closer to have a look at it and you notice ancient paintings. Most of them depict a beautiful naked woman with reptilian eyes and a serpent's tail. You can also see characters and symbols there.

Suddenly you hear a whisper. You turn around and you can see a black-haired woman looking at you. With a gesture she invites you to come closer, points at the ruby and hands you a dagger. She opens her mouth and speaks the language of the serpents but you can understand her words: "make a sacrifice for our mother Lilith and gaze into the stone." She leaves and you stay alone. You cut your left hand with the dagger and pour the blood on the ruby altar. There you also put the dagger. You gaze into the jewel and absorb the visions. The goddess will show you her seal with which you will be able to find her again in your dreams. When the vision ends, slowly return to your normal consciousness.

Sorath – Steiner's View of the Antichrist

Asenath Mason

"But there is also an opposing principle to the Lamb: there is the Sun Demon, the so-called Demon of the Sun, that which works in the evil forces of man, thrusting back the force of the Lamb. It works in such a way that certain portion of the human race will be excluded from the evolution leading to the Sun."[16]

In 1908, Rudolf Steiner held a series of lectures on the Apocalypse, the Antichrist and the opposing forces of good and evil. The central figure of these lectures was the so-called Sun Demon Sorath. Traditionally, Sorath is known as the spirit of the Sun, the dark counterpart of Archangel Michael, and his name translates as "the banished one." Therefore, he is an "evil angel," the dark spirit who rules not the Sun itself but rather its dark side, the Black Sun. In the Qabalah, he is the intelligence of Thagirion, the Qliphothic counterpart of Tipheret. In his theories, Steiner came to identify Sorath with the force opposing Christ, the Christ's Shadow, the Antichrist. The Biblical Apocalypse speaks of three beasts: the great red dragon with 7 heads, 10 horns and 7 crowns; a sea beast with 7 heads, 10 horns and 10 crowns; and finally – an earth beast with two horns

---

[16] Rudolf Steiner's lectures

which looks like a lamb but speaks like a dragon.[17] That last beast is Sorath, the spirit whose number is 666, the one whose aim is to destroy the work of Christ.

Steiner explains the significance of the name Sorath (s-v-r-t) and its numerical value in the following way: the letter Samech stands for the physical body, Vau – the etheric body, Resh – the astral body, and Tau – the lower "I" – all of these refer to man. Sorath is therefore inseparably connected with a human being as an integral part of the Self. What is significant – he represents the lower aspects of the Self, the ones connected with the earth, and also with the ego. Steiner claimed that during the Apocalypse the activity of Sorath would be revealed in the "War of All against All," which means a misguided ego development, or the obsession with the "I." In Steiner's view, this will not happen soon – the earth is still in the process of evolution, the process that includes seven great stages that will come to an end in a distant future. Then, mankind will be faced with the choice between Christ and Antichrist, the Lamb and the Beast. However, Sorath is inherent in the human Self and thus never ceases to be active "in evil forces of man." His influence is continuous and inevitable, and it is expressed in basic instincts, impulses and lower actions of the will ("Mankind has a thorn in the flesh" – 2 Corinthians 12:2). The consequence of this is the lack of need for spiritualization, which creates a void that is filled with an urge to extreme experiences arising from instincts: sexual perversions, senseless violence, drug abuse, etc. (actually, the recognizable symptoms of our times). Thus, humanity does not progress spiritually but relies solely on a momentary gratification of the bodily needs. That is why

---

[17] Terry Boardman: *Aspects of the Occult Significance of the Year 1998*

Steiner called Sorath "the arch-enemy of all development" and "the denier of all change."[18]

Identification with Sorath leads to an illusory conviction that one is a god. From this conviction arises the denial of spiritual progress and the illusive sense of strength:

"But the aim of being who hoped to intervene in 666 was to make himself God. That means, he wanted to take place of God for mankind; he was filled with what constitutes the Antichrist. This is expressed in the self-deification tendency of some dictators of the twentieth century."[19]

Steiner refers here to the year 666 when the teachings inspired by Sorath were about to spread all over Europe from the academy of Gondishapur. He even mentions a teacher from Gondishapur "whose name is unknown, but who was the greatest opponent of Christ Jesus."[20] The self-deification tendency he speaks about means not the path of progress but a mere identification with the ego and rejection of spirituality that is concealed from man who "remains an animal, lags behind in his human evolution."[21] This results first in stagnation, then in regression. To illustrate this denial of the spirit, Steiner refers to the Eighth Ecumenical Council of 869, when, according to him, the spirit was abolished. In his view, this event that influenced the further tendencies in Christianity was inspired by Sorath:

"The being who hoped to intervene in 666 said: 'Men will come who no longer direct their gaze to the spirit – the spirit will not interest them. I shall see to it' (and this he

---

[18] Rudolf Steiner's lectures
[19] Ibid.
[20] Ibid.
[21] Ibid.

actually brought about) that in the year 869 a Council will be held in Constantinople at which the spirit will be abolished. Men will no longer be interested in the spirit; they will turn their attention to nature and form ghostlike concepts of nature."[22]

And is it not what actually happened to Christianity in the following centuries? The general manifestation of the Sorath principle triggered the tendency to deny and reject the spirit that characterizes the gradual development of the Christian doctrine. In this case, it is interesting to follow Steiner's theory that evolutionary streams in Christianity have been the work of the Antichrist.

The symbolic sign of Sorath is a stroke bent back, with two curved points:

The curved branches represent two horns of the Beast. They are also symbolic of two "chief servants" of Sorath – Lucifer and Ahriman, the force of light and the essence of darkness, wisdom and strength. In Steiner's view, Sorath stands behind Lucifer and Ahriman and inspires their actions. Steiner claimed that they both had or would have

---

[22] Ibid.

the period in history when their manifestation would reach its climax. According to this view, Lucifer had already ruled the earth – in the third millennium BCE when he incarnated in China. Ahriman is yet about to be incarnated, which should happen in the West at the end of the second millennium CE. Following this idea, we might assume that his incarnation in the flesh has already occurred, and the period from 2000 CE onwards will be dominated by Ahrimanic emanations. Lucifer's incarnation marked the so-called period of man's incarnation into physical existence, Ahriman's – the time of excarnation out of physical existence. Ahriman has been trying to prevent this spiritual excarnation of human beings. In relation to Lucifer, he might be called the spirit of contraction, while the "Light-Bearer" represents the principle of spiritual expansion. Sorath is behind both of these principles. He does not incarnate but remains hidden and unknown like a shadow. Steiner often refers to him as the Shadow of Christ, and emphasizes that the primary aim of Sorath is to destroy what Christ has done for mankind. Thus, the focus of his activity is on the lower instincts of man and the ego, where lies the greatest potential of Sorathic principle, this "thorn in the flesh:"

"For this War of All against All is the result of the 'kink' left behind in the physical body as the remains of Sorath's activity, the 'thorn' that can really lead to an incitement of the body-bound instinctive forces of egoism, which are so powerful because they are rooted undetected in the unconscious will of man."[23]

This turn toward instincts, urges and impulses prepares the ground for Ahrimanic influence. Moreover, as Sorath's

---

[23] Peter Tradowsky: *Christ and Antichrist - Understanding The Events At The End Of The Century*

activity focuses on materialism, his other major tool is the god of money, Mammon. The period of Ahriman is also the time of Mammon's rule over the world. Everything is purchasable and money is put above mankind – it is more important than the human being. Humanity is trapped in the pursuit of an empty illusion. In Steiner's view, this is characteristic of Sorath's activity – the focus on earth and matter.

According to Peter Tradowsky, who wrote about Steiner's theories in his book *Christ and Antichrist*, the most evident example of Sorathic possession was Hitler and the whole Nazi movement, the symbol of which was the swastika, the ancient representation of the Sun. It is significant that Hitler was convinced of his absolute power and wanted to be accepted almost as a god. His obsessive fanaticism about a unified state ("one people, one Empire, one leader") was an expression of this aspiration. A striking instance of the manifestation of Sorathic principle was his statement: "The work begun by Christ, I will bring to a conclusion!" – declaration in which he puts himself in the place of the Antichrist. Another Sorathic quality was Hitler's amazing ability to manipulate the audience. His opponents went to meetings with counter-arguments and returned as enthusiastic supporters of his policies. He had an incredible skill of paralyzing thoughts of crowds – thus creating the mind hypnosis, the gateway for Sorath to enter. His speeches stirred the crowd so extremely that people were totally overwhelmed with love, adoration, enthusiasm, fury – feelings so intense that brought them to tears. He possessed a strange magnetism, the ability to enter the will of others, as if he "put them under a spell." What is interesting, even at the moments of passionate speeches, he kept his own emotions in a firm grip: "When he flung his tirades of hate into the auditorium, he was at the same time in control of his ebullition." This combination of fanaticism with rationality is the perfect example of what Steiner called the collaboration of Lucifer and Ahriman. It is also significant that little was known about Hitler's personality – a typical example of Sorath's desire to remain as an unknown shadow. Even his close advisors could say very little about him. As Ribbentrop writes:

"The fact is that, although I have experienced so much with him, I have not got any closer to him humanly or otherwise in all our years of working together than I was on the first day we were acquainted."[24]

There was one more striking resemblance to Sorath's striving to be regarded as God – the use of the "heil" salute. As Tradowsky observes, this word in German language had been so far used only with reference to God or something divine.

Even though anthroposophy called the year 1933 "the rise of the Beast," Steiner believed that the peak of Sorath's influence occurs every 666 years in earth evolution. On such occasions the Antichrist attempts to enter the minds of humans and lead them away from Christ. For the first time such an attempt took place in the year 666 when Sorath was about to give mankind knowledge for which people were not ready (the conscious soul), which could have catastrophic results for humanity. The tool of the Beast was then the Academy in Gondishapur in Persia. The next occurrence of 666 happened in 1332, the year of Black Death and other disastrous events. The third occurrence took place in 1998 which, according to Steiner, was the rise of Ahrimanic rule over the earth. Steiner held his lectures concerning the end of the millennium long before 1998. He was not mistaken, however, as to the omnipresent authority of materialism and ego-obsession. Much of his

---

[24] Ibid.

theories fit the present world-picture – concentration on earthly aspects of life.

Sorath is therefore not as much of a "Sun demon" as an "earth demon," the beast that emerges from the earth and rules the earth. However, his emanation does not mean the total rejection of spiritual forces but rather their different use: the descent instead of the ascent. In modern esotericism, this is the distinction underlying two spiritual attitudes: the Right Hand Path and the Left Hand Path. For the Right Hand Path, the force of the "I," the ego, is dangerous and is a mere hindrance in the spiritual progress. The Left Hand Path exploits the ego power and views it as a potential. This practice throughout ages has been known as black magic. Aleister Crowley referred to magicians who used the ego force as "the black brothers," the opposite of "the white brotherhood" whose aim was to leave the ego behind on the spiritual path. That is the reason underlying Steiner's conviction that Sorath leads man into black magic:

"Ultimately mankind will become divided into those who use white magic and those who use black magic. Thus in the mystery of 666, or Sorath is hidden the secret of black magic."[25]

There is a theory that the name "Sorath" can be derived from Suriel/Sarhapanim, the female form of which is Suriath. This was originally an angel whose task was to guard the sunlight during the night and return it to God in the morning. This motif of the Sun at night appears in all cultures and is known as the Dark Sun, the Black Sun, or the Sun in Darkness. If we follow Steiner's view that Christ was the Sun, then logically Sorath as the Antichrist is the Black Sun – and as the upward ascent toward Christ is

---

[25] Rudolf Steiner's lectures

characteristic of the Right Hand Path, the descent toward the Sun in Darkness is the essence of the Left Hand Path.

There is a difference, however, between being an unconscious vessel for Sorathic powers and the conscious use of them which is characteristic of the Left Hand Path currents. The path of self-deification is based not on the mere illusion of "being a god," the vessel for the Antichrist, but the striving to become the Adversary oneself, the self-isolated consciousness. This is the attitude toward progress under the sign of the inner Sun, the Black Sun that is represented by Sorath.

Bibliography:

1. Peter Tradowsky: *Christ and Antichrist - Understanding The Events At The End Of The Century*
2. Terry Boardman: *Aspects of the Occult Significance of the Year 1998*
3. Rudolf Steiner's lectures

The Fall of Lucifer
Gustave Doré, XIX century

About the Publisher

Draco Press is a new aeon publisher of quality books of Luciferian philosophy and practices. It is our mission to provide resources that are steeped in application and founded on solid principles. We believe in promoting freedom of thought, and the freedom of individual growth and development through spiritual practices in line with Luciferian principles. In our context, Lucifer is the Light Bringer, and it is from this perspective we do our part to bring more light into a world in transition. Founded by Asenath Mason and Bill Duvendack in 2018, Draco Press endeavors to bring quality authors and books into mass consciousness.

www.dracopress.com

Temple of Ascending Flame

TEMPLE of Ascending Flame is a platform for individuals around the world who want to share certain aspects of their work within the Draconian Gnosis with other adepts of the path and for those who simply need guidance into Draconian initiatory magic. It is both for newcomers who make their first steps on the Path of the Dragon and for experienced individuals who wish to progress on the Left Hand Path. We are not a "magical order." We do not charge fees for membership and our work is not based on any hierarchies. There are no restrictions on participation in our open projects, and in our inner work we welcome all who are capable of receiving and channeling the gnosis of the Dragon.

More information: ascendingflame.com
Contact: info@ascendingflame.com

Made in the USA
Columbia, SC
19 December 2019